9000 NEW SCRAPBOOK TITLES!

NEVER BE AT A LOSS FOR A PAGE TITLE AGAIN!

BY
KATHY BOYERS

9000 NEW SCRAPBOOK TITLES!

copyright © 2009 by Kathy Boyers.
All rights reserved.
No part of this book may be reproduced
in any form without the prior permission
of the author.

For information, write:

Kathy Boyers
14156 Evergreen Trail
Manitou Beach, MI 49253
www.9000scrapbooktitles.com

ISBN: 978-0-557-13574-5

Published by:
Lulu.com
September, 2009

Dedication

This book is dedicated to my husband, Bob.
He always believes in me,
no matter what zany idea I come up with.
This book would not have been written
without his encouragement.

And also to my great friend, Dawn,
who came up with some fantastic title ideas,
and generously let me use them in this book.

(Font: Hollywierd LET)

Introduction

(Font: Swiss 721 SWA)

Contrary to what many people believe, scrapbooking is so much more than just a hobby. It fulfills so many needs. It's a way to express ourselves and our feelings; it is an outlet for our artistic abilities; It's a way to preserve the past; and it is also a way to record our lives today, for future generations. Whatever the reason you scrapbook, it is a satisfying and rewarding endeavor.

But, I find it a REAL challenge to keep my pages looking fresh and new. It is very easy to fall into a pattern that is comfortable. But, by doing so, those same pages may begin to look repetitive, and lack interest.

One of the easiest ways to capture your reader's attention, is to use imaginative and refreshing titles. Many page titles simply state what is happening in the photos. This common practice may lead to pages that tend to get stale. By using titles that are out of the ordinary, your work will stay fresh and appealing.

For example, when creating a page about your child's bath, it is easy to fall into the pattern of using a title that just states what is going on in the photos, such as "BATH TIME". This title does not really grab the reader's attention. Why not mix things up a little, and use a title that will really intrigue the reader. You could use "THE NAKED TRUTH", or "HONEY, I SHRUNK THE KIDS!" Clever titles like these, will draw the person enjoying your scrapbooks into the page, and make them want to look further.

Another way to add variety, is to vary your fonts. Notice that throughout this book, many different fonts are used. The font name appears under each category. Many of these fonts come with the popular software programs. If the fonts you are interested in are not included in your program, I suggest you do a search on the internet for them.

There is also an index in the back of this book, which includes hundreds of descriptive words that will help you to express yourself in both your titles and your journaling.

This book is a compilation of new and fresh titles. While I cannot guarantee that you have not seen these titles before, I do guarantee that there are tons of new ideas in every category.

I hope you enjoy using this book as much as I have enjoyed writing it.

TABLE OF CONTENTS

(FONT: STENCIL BT)

TOP TEN TIPS FOR
TERRIFIC TITLES......... 9

ANYTIME TITLES.......... 11

ARMED FORCES............ 12

BABIES...................... 13
    BABY PICTURES...... 15
    BABY PLAY............. 15
    CHANGING DIAPERS. 16
    FEEDING BABY........ 16
    NAP TIME................ 16

BIRTHDAYS................. 17

BOOKS....................... 17

BUGS......................... 18

CARD GAMES.............. 19

CARS......................... 19

COLLECTORS............... 20

COMPUTERS................ 20

CRYING...................... 21

DANCE....................... 22

EXERCISE................... 23

EYES......................... 24
    GLASSES................ 24

FAMILY...................... 25

AUNT........................ 26
BROTHER................... 26
DAD.......................... 26
    DADSPEAK.......... 27
DAUGHTER................. 27
GRANDCHILDREN.... 27
GRANDPARENTS..... 28
MOM......................... 28
    MOMSPEAK.......... 29
PARENTS................... 29
SISTER...................... 29
SON.......................... 29

FIREWORKS................ 30

FOOD......................... 30
    BAKING................. 31
    COOKING............... 31
    GRILLING.............. 32

FRIENDS..................... 33

FROGS....................... 34

GAMBLING.................. 35

GARDENING................ 36

GROWING OLDER......... 38

HAIR.......................... 39

HAPPINESS................. 39

HATS......................... 40

HERITAGE.................. 40

HOBBIES................. 41	LOVE....................... 65
NEEDLECRAFTS...... 42	LOVER'S SPATS...... 67
CROSS STITCH........ 42	LOVING YOU........... 68
QUILTING............... 42	
PHOTOGRAPHY....... 43	MARRIAGE................. 70
SCRAPBOOKING...... 43	WEDDINGS.............. 71
STAINED GLASS...... 44	
STAMPING............... 45	MEMORIES................... 72
WOODWORKING...... 45	
	MEN........................... 73
HOLIDAYS................... 46	MEN AND HAIR........ 75
CHRISTMAS............ 46	MEN AND TOOLS...... 75
EASTER.................. 47	
HALLOWEEN........... 48	MUSIC........................ 76
THANKSGIVING....... 48	MUSIC MAKERS....... 76
HOME......................... 49	NATURE...................... 77
HOME MAINT.......... 49	
HOUSEWORK........... 50	PETS.......................... 78
NEW HOME............... 50	BIRDS..................... 81
BUYING A HOME. 51	CATS...................... 82
NEW HOME CONST.. 51	KITTENS............. 82
YARD WORK....... 51	DOGS...................... 83
	PUPPIES............. 83
HUGS.......................... 52	FERRETS................ 84
	HAMSTERS............. 84
INSPIRATION................ 52	HORSES................. 84
	IGUANAS................ 85
KIDS.......................... 54	RABBITS................ 85
BATH TIME.............. 56	SNAKES................. 85
BOYS...................... 56	
CHILD'S PLAY......... 57	PREGNANCY................ 86
GIRLS..................... 59	
KIDS AND BABIES... 60	PROFESSIONS.............. 87
KIDS AND PETS....... 60	ACCOUNTANT......... 88
KIDS & PREGNANCY 60	ASTRONOMER......... 88
KIDSPEAK............... 60	CARPENTER........... 88
NAP TIME............... 61	CLOCK REPAIRMAN 89
POTTY TRAINING.... 62	COMPUTER TECH.... 89
TWINS.................... 62	DENTIST................. 89
	ELECTRICIAN.......... 90
KITE FLYING................ 63	ENGINEER............... 90
	EXTERMINATOR...... 90
LAUGHTER................... 63	FACTORY WORKER 91
	FARMER................. 91
LIFE........................... 64	FIREFIGHTER......... 92

HAIRDRESSER	92	AUTO RACING	113
JEWELER	93	BOXING	114
JUDGE	93	FENCING	114
LAB TECHNICIAN	93	GOLF	114
LAWYER	94	KARATE	115
MANAGER	94	SKATEBOARDING	115
MECHANIC	94	TEAM SPORTS	115
MINISTER	94	BASEBALL	115
NURSE	95	BASKETBALL	116
PAINTER	95	BOWLING	116
PHYSICIAN	96	CHEERLEADING	116
PILOT	96	COACHING	116
POLICE OFFICER	97	DIVING	117
PRISON GUARD	97	FOOTBALL	117
PSYCHOLOGIST	97	GYMNASTICS	117
SECRETARY	98	HOCKEY	118
STORE CLERK	98	SOCCER	118
TATTOO ARTIST	98	SWIMMING	118
TEACHER	99	TENNIS	118
TRAIN ENGINEER	99	TRACK & FIELD	119
TRUCK DRIVER	99	VOLLEYBALL	119
VETERINARIAN	100	WEIGHT LIFTING	119
WAITER/WAITRESS	100	WRESTLING	119
		WILDERNESS SPORTS	120
RELAXATION	101	ARCHERY	120
		BOATING	121
SCHOOL	102	CANOEING	121
COLLEGE	103	FISHING	122
GRADUATION	104	FOUR WHEELING	123
SCHOOL DANCE	104	HIKING	123
		HOT AIR BALLOON	123
SEASONS	105	HUNTING	124
FALL	105	ICE SKATING	125
SPRING	105	MOTORCYCLES &	
SUMMER	106	DIRT BIKES	125
AT THE POOL	107	ROCK CLIMBING	125
SUN TANNING	107	SKY DIVING	126
WINTER	108	SNOW SKIING	126
		SNOWMOBILING	126
SHOPPING	109	SPELUNKING	127
		SURFING	127
SLEEP	109	WATER SKIING	127
SMILES	110	TEENS	128
SPORTS	111	THEATER	132

TRAVEL	132	WORSHIP	147
AIR TRAVEL	134		
ROAD TRIP	134	YOUNG ADULTS	148
VACATION	134	ZOO	152
AMUSEMENT PARKS	136	FEEDING TIME	154
AT THE BEACH	137		
CAMPING	138	MISCELLANEOUS TITLES	155
CAMPFIRES	140		
CRUISE	140	INDEX	
		DESCRIPTIVE WORDS	156
VOLUNTEERISM	142		
WEATHER	142	YOUR FAVORITE TITLES	169
WEIGHT	143		
WOMEN	144	PAGE IDEAS	170
WOODCUTTING	147		

TOP TEN TIPS
FOR
TERRIFIC TITLES

(Font: Americana BT)

1) One of the easiest ways to spice up a title is to vary the fonts or stickers used. I recommend that you use no more than three different fonts, stickers, or colors per page. Using more than three choices can make your titles and journaling difficult to read.

2) Distort fonts using Photoshop or whichever software program to which you have access. A font can be stretched in all different directions. It can be given drop shadows, a chrome look, a variety of colors, and many other unique looks. Explore your software program and use it to it's fullest extent.

3) Vary the placement of the title on your page. Don't be afraid to put it in the middle of the page, on the bottom, or down either side. Also, don't be afraid to let it bleed over onto a photo, especially if there is a lot of area in the photo that is not needed to convey the feeling of the page. It is also a good way to cover up a small part of a photo that you do not want showing, like the back of someone's head.

4) Use color to make a title pop off the page. One of my favorite tricks, is to match the color of the title to a main color in the focal photo. It ties your page together nicely. If the color does not look good on the background paper, simply mat the title with a neutral color first.

5) Match the mood of your font or stickers to the feeling you're trying to convey on the page. If you're going for a page that is soft and cuddly, you might want to use Mulberry or a pastel color of paper. For a man's page, metal, wood, or rustic papers work well.

6) Cut letters for titles out of unexpected items, such as cork for a man's or student's page. Foil, material, and photo scraps are other interesting items to use. Look around your home. You may find something that you have never considered using before. If you're worried about the acid content of an item, you can purchase a pen that will test the acidity of the item.

7) Decorate letters with stickers, paint, etc. This is a very quick way to spice up your title. Letters look good with small flower stickers draped over parts of them. Cartoon characters peeking from around the letters are also cute. A little paint gives the letters texture. Other items to use include ink, chalks for shading, stamps, etc.

8) Use letter stickers as a mask. Paint over the stickers, and then peel the stickers off to reveal your title. This works great if you don't have the right letters in a particular color of stickers to complete your title.

9) Personalize your titles whenever possible. Instead of "Senior Trip", include the person's name with the title. For example, "Kathy's Amazing Senior Trip" is much more interesting. Using favorite nicknames is also a great way to personalize. If you decide to use a nickname, don't forget to include in your journaling, how the nickname came about.

10) Use motto's and sayings from brochures, and maps. Professionals are paid huge amounts of money to come up with clever slogans for places of interest. State and school mottoes are also great choices. What better title could there be for your pages?

Inspiration for titles can come from anywhere; song titles, book titles, magazine articles, and slang terms are just a few of the places you can find great titles. But, listen to the voice of experience. When you come across a great title idea, write it down in the back of this book in the area provided. If you don't, you'll never think of it when you're ready to scrapbook those great pages.

Happy Scrapping!

Anytime Titles

(Font: GoudyOldSty T)

_____ is cheaper than a psychiatrist
A good day
A good year
A tribute to _____
ADD – Another Disorganized Day
Adventures of _____
All about _____
All about me
All about you
All I ever wanted
American dreams
Beyond expectations
Can't live without it
Can't live without them/you
Claim to fame
Delightful days
Delightful diversion
Eat, drink, _____
Entertainment tonight
Favorite pastime
Food for thought
For your amusement
For your entertainment
Going places
Good news
Good times
Hooked on _____
I look up to you
In motion

Indulge in the things you love
Into the wild
It happens every day
I've got personality
Just hangin' out
Like no other
Mastering the skill of _____
"Me" time
Peaceful pastime
Perfect pictures/photos
Photo op
Pleasant pursuit
Source of endless pleasure
The adventures of _____
The beauty of _____
The big day
The good life
The joy of _____
The sweet life
Things that really matter
Tons of fun
What a great _____ looks like
When in doubt, _____
You are my hero
You are my inspiration
"You"nique
"You"niquely you
You're very photogenic
You've got personality

Armed Forces

(Font: Copperplate)

- A life altering experience
- A lifetime of service
- A man/woman of Honor
- A tribute to _____
- Action heroes
- Aim high
- Air male
- American Gladiators
- An officer and a gentleman
- And liberty for all
- Army times
- Be a leader
- Be all you can be
- Born free, and determined to stay that way
- Bring our troops home
- Built tough
- Courage isn't the lack of fear, it's controlling your fears
- Defender of freedom
- Desperate times, desperate Measures
- Fighting for freedom
- Fighting to stay free
- For love and glory
- For the love of country
- Freedom forever
- Freedom isn't free
- Genuine American hero
- Good morning Vietnam
- Good morning _____
- Great American hero
- Guardians of freedom
- Have gun will travel
- Helmet hair
- Hero worship
- Heroes never die
- History makers
- Hooray for heroes
- I am my brother's keeper
- In step
- In the company of soldiers
- Journey to Freedom
- Keep him/her safe
- Keeping us safe
- League of gentlemen /women
- Letter from home
- Make peace, not war
- Making a difference
- Man/woman behind the uniform
- May freedom be forever
- My hero/Heroine
- Navy times
- None braver
- Peacemakers
- Please God, bring him/her home safe
- Please God, bring us peace
- Real heroes
- Real heroes are hard to find
- Real life heroes
- Risking their safety for ours
- Seek and destroy
- Shaping his/her future
- Silent knights
- Soldiers for freedom
- Striving for excellence
- The defenders
- The incredibles
- The intimidators
- The road to victory
- Today's heroes
- Top notch
- Tough Stuff
- True blue hero
- True calling
- True heroes earn respect
- Veterans are valuable
- Watch over him/her
- What a great soldier looks like
- Young American

Babies

(Font: Pink LET)

A brand new life
A child is born
A little glimpse of heaven
After birth
All we ever wanted
All we'll ever need
Ain't he/she sweet?
American baby
An angel from the start
And the story begins
Angel baby
Angels on earth
Aren't I cute?
Babies are fringe benefits
Babies are little pieces of heaven
Babies crawl into your heart
Baby meets world
Baby talk
Baby, you smell sooo good
Blessed/Bright beginnings
Born to be loved
Can't get enough of you
Center of our universe
Child bearing
Child of God
Child of my heart
Complete Angel
Couldn't live without you
Crazy for you
Cute character
Cute little creation
Delightful dream
Designed by us/God
Drooling over you
Everybody loves _____
First born
Future American Idol
God's little miracle
Good day, sunshine
Good things come in small packages
Growing like a weed
Handle with care
He's/She's a miracle
He's/she's creating a storm
He's/she's here to stay
He's/she's the real thing
High maintenance
Hold on to this moment
Home made
Homemade happiness
I am baby, watch me grow
If I could save time in a bottle
I'm here!
In good hands
It's a miracle!
It's all about you
It's so nice to be with you
Just as long as we have you
Keep him/her safe
King/Queen of cuddle
Kisses are messengers of love
Lap land
Like no other
Little masterpiece/seedling
Little nursery man
Little sport/swinger
Losing sleep over you
Love at first sigh
Mad about you
Made in America
Male delivery
Mild child

Million dollar baby
Miracle from God
Modern marvel
Most wanted
My baby loves me
My special angel
My teddy bear and my pacifier,
    they comfort me
My world, and welcome to it
Nature's best
New beginnings
Newcomer
No greater joy
Oh, baby!
Oh so charming
Oh, what a beautiful baby
One day at a time
Only the best for you
Our awesome accomplishment
Our favorite place to be is
    next to you
Our little offspring/pacifist
Our silver lining
Our special angel
Out of this world
Perfect love/moments
Proof of heaven's existence
Purely you
Remarkable you
Right from the heart
Rock-a-bye baby
Rock around the clock
Rockin' the night away
Ruler of the roost
Secret language of babies
Showered with love
Simply sensational
Small wonder
Smallville
So blessed to have you
Something so sweet

Super baby
Super little human
Sweet greetings
Sweet little seedling/sensation
Sweet little valentine
Sweet smiles/stuff
Sweet young thing
Tale of the tooth
Ten tiny toes
The baby with something extra
The beauty of baby
The heart of the matter
The joy a child brings
The next generation
The sun rises in your eyes
The wonder of babies
Then came you
Thousands of possibilities
    await you
Three's company
'Till the end of time
Tiny souls
To baby with love
Together we can do anything
Touched by an angel
Treasure from the heart
Unconditional love
Watch over him/her
We had a dream, and you came
    true
We love all you do
We will always be there
We're with you always
What a cutie!
What a little flirt
What a sweetheart/sweetie!
What I like/love about you
What matters most
When in doubt, hold/rock a baby
When in doubt, kiss a baby
When you were born

Will wonders never cease?
Wonder of life/love
You are here
You are so beautiful to me
You are the center of our universe
You fill my life with smiles
You light up my life
You make everything/life worthwhile
You make life wonderful/worth living
You make us happy
You touch my heart

You'll always be my baby
Young American
Young one
You're adorable/captivating
You're charming/grrreat!
You're in good hands
You're one of a kind
You're the boss
You're the greatest
You're the one
You're the world to me
You're worth it!
You've changed our lives forever

Baby pictures

Aren't I cute?
MVP - Most Valuable Picture
Personality portrait
Photo op

Precious little body parts
Precious portraits
You ought to be in pictures
You're very photogenic

Baby Play

Busy baby
Busy body
Carpet cruiser
Crawl space
Don't fence me in
Floor crawler
Four on the floor
I am baby, watch me crawl
Kid rock

King/Queen of the carpet
Life behind bars
Little playpen men
Little playpen pals
Ruler of the playpen
Shake, rattle, and roll
Step by step
Sweet little swinger
Treasured teddy

Changing diapers

A changing experience
A filling experience
Baby, you smell soooo bad!
Changing times
Check 'n' go - a tip for those who change diapers
Diaper doo/duo
Doo it right
Every path has it's puddle
Fill 'er up
Full of fun
Keep him covered
Leave your mark
May your diapers always be dry
Mr./Miss messy pants
Slip, slidin' away

Feeding baby

A filling experience
Bottle baby
Can't get enough
Chow down/hound
Feed me faster
Lactation station
Lip smackin' good
May your bottle always be warm
Mom learns the real meaning of "feed back"
Spit happens
Sticky fingers

Nap time

All tuckered out
Boy cot
Cat nap
Catching some ZZZ's
Cradle song
Crib notes
Dark room
Delightful dreams
Down time
Dozer
Dream happy, little one
Dream maker/catcher
Dream weaver
Dreamscapes
Eat, drink, sleep
Go to sleep my darling
Kid napper
Kiddy winks
Land of nod
Night owl
Quiet moments
Silent nights
Sleeping Beauty
Sleeping the night away
Sleepy eyes/head
Sleepy/Slumber time
Sounds of silence
Tales from the crib
The napster
While you were sleeping

Birthdays

(Font: Zaragoza LET)

A world of wishes
Age doesn't matter
Another banner year
Birthday babe/boy
Celebrating the day you blessed/ brightened our world
Celebrating the person you are
Don't count years –count memories
Eventful eighties
Fabulous forties/fifties
Fantastic forties/fifties
Father's/Mother's day
Fun forties/fifties
Getting together
Growing up too fast
Happy birthday baby
Many happy returns
May all your wishes be granted
Nimble nineties
One cannot have too large a party
Ornery octogenarian
Outgoing octogenarian
Party at the park
Party hearty
Pass the presents
Prince/Princess of the party
Seize the day
Sixteen candles
So many candles so little breath/time
"Son" day
That dangerous age
The big day
The ice cream was chilling
The party's over
This one's for you!
What's a birthday without cake?
You take the cake
You're worth it!

Books

(Font: Book Antiqua)

A book lets you go any-
    where and be anything
A novel idea
A real page turner
Book boy/babe
Book keeper
Book nook
Book store – my favorite
    place to shop
Bookery

Books - don't leave home without them
Books 'R' us
Brain work
Can't get enough
Concentration
Curious minds
Delightful diversion
Expand your mind
Explore new frontiers
Fact or fiction
Favorite pastime
Fiction fan
I cannot live without books
Ideas ahead
Mastering the skill of reading
May your book light always shine bright
Non-fiction fan
Passport to adventure
Peaceful pastime
Pleasant pursuit
Read between the pines
Reading under cover
To learn to read is to expand the mind
To learn to read is to open new worlds
Tools for success
What's reading without imagination
Where information lives
Your ticket to the world

Bugs

(Font: Chipper LET)

Back to nature
Beautiful butterflies
Bees are "hum" bugs
Bug boy/babe
Buzzers
Buzzy bodies
Communing with nature
Creepy crawlers
Custom sound
Designed by Mother Nature
Fact or fiction
Flutter-bys
How to catch bugs
In motion
Into the wild
Intriguing insects

Lightening bugs are nature's
　　nightlights
May your bug spray always
　　be handy
Small wonders

Spiders are web crawlers
Spiders surfing the web
Stranger than fiction
The lively bunch
The secret world of bugs

Card games

(Font: Comic Sans MS)

All bets are off
Ante up
Card shark
Claim to fame
Deal me in
Eat, drink, play cards
Favorite pastime

Guy's/Girl's club
Miss/Ms. lucky
Mr./Mrs. lucky
Penny ante poker
Play boy/girl
Poker face
Poker pals/party

CARS

(Font: STOP)

ALL WASHED UP
IN MOTION
MAN AND MACHINE
AMERICAN MUSCLE CAR
AUTO ZONE
BUILT TOUGH
BUBBLES AND SHINES
BURN RUBBER
CAR AND DRIVER
CAR COLLECTOR
CAR CRAFT
CAR TUNES
CRUISE AMERICA
CRUISIN' IN MY CAR
CUSTOM MACHINES
MAY YOUR TANK ALWAYS BE
　　FULL

DESIGNED BY _____
DEVIL ON WHEELS
FASTER THAN A SPEEDING
　　BULLET
FIRST SET OF WHEELS
FOUR ON THE FLOOR
GETTING A TUNE UP
GOING PLACES
GOT WHEELS?
HOT ROD GIRL/GUY
IN MOTION
JUST CRUISIN'
MAN AND MACHINE
MAN OVER MACHINE
PASSPORT TO ADVENTURE
SLIP, SLIDIN' AWAY
MODERN MARVELS

MOTOR MADNESS
MOTOR MAMA/MAN
MOTOR MANIA
MY CAR MOVES ME
MY PRIDE AND JOY
MY TURN TO DRIVE
NO STOPPING ME NOW

SOURCE OF ENDLESS PLEASURE
TEARING UP THE TREAD/TRAIL
THE PRICE IS RIGHT
TICKET TO RIDE
WHEEL LIFE
YOUNG RIDERS
ZOOM, ZOOM, ZOOM

Collectors

(Font: CAC Saxon Bold)

(what you collect) appreciation
_____ collector extraordinaire
_____ fan/mania
Can't get enough
Claim to fame
Cool collectables
Cool collections/collectors
Delightful diversions
Do your own thing
Everything has beauty
Hidden treasures
I collect _____

I'm a _____ collector
Indulge in the things you
  truly love
Set high standards
So many _____, so little
  money
Treasure hunt
What a cool collector looks like
What a find!
You can never have too many
  _____

Computers

[Font: Data Seventy LET]

Computer corner
Computer genius/whiz
Computer kid
Crazy for computers
Do things you think you
  cannot
Do your own thing
Eat, drink, surf the web
Favorite pastime
Go anywhere, be anything
High tech

I suffer from OCD –
  Obsessive computer
  disorder
Ideas ahead
Keys to success
Lead the way
Let the games begin
Nintendo power
Passport to adventure
Play on
PlayStation power

Shape your future
So many games, so little time
Tech time
Technically speaking
Tools for success
True calling
Terminal techie
Thousands of possibilities
 await you
True techie
Try something new
Where information lives
Whiz kids
Wired
Yes you can
Your ticket to the world

Crying

(Font: Arriba LET)

_____ sings the blues
Baby sings the blues
Bawl room
Brother/sister sings
 the blues
Cry baby, cry
Crying over you
Custom sound
Daytime drama
Don't cry
Every path has a puddle
I am baby, hear me cry
Make yourself heard
Mama/papa sings the blues
May your Kleenex
 always be handy
"Me" time
Sad sack
Tears happen
Tears of happiness
Tears of joy
Tearful times
Tearful tot
That had to hurt!
Trail of tears
Waa, waa,, waa
Waterworks

Dance

(Font: Dancin LET)

Agony of the feet
Aim high
All tapped out
At the hop, hop, hop
Busy body
Can't live without it
Claim to fame
Could I have this dance?
Create a storm
Dance spirit/steps
Dancin' in he dark/moonlight
Delightful diversion
Determination
Do your own thing
Dramatic dancer
Encore, encore
Endless energy supply
Exceed your dreams
Foot man
Foot worn
Fred Astaire, I'm not
Ginger Rogers, I'm not
Happy feet
Have it your way
High hopes
I believe in me
I hope you dance
In motion
In step
Indulge in the things you truly love
It's time for a foot rest
Just dance
Lead the way
Let the music move you
Let's see what you can do
Music moves me
Music sets my soul on fire
Music stirs my soul
No stopping me now
Nobody does it better
Party line dancing
Passion to perform
Pursue perfection
Shall we dance?
Source of endless pleasure
Stand out in a crowd
Step by step
Still standing
Stomping grounds
Strive for excellence
That had to hurt
The lively bunch
The music scene
These shoes are made for dancing
Thousands of possibilities await you
Try something new
True calling
Tuff stuff
Twinkle toes
What's dance without music?
When in doubt, dance

Exercise

(DellaRobbia BT)

- Aim high
- Anything's possible
- Be fearless
- Built tough
- Bun Control
- Busy body
- Can't get enough
- Can't live without it
- Desperate measures
- Determination
- Do it best
- Do it right
- Do more
- Don't quit!
- Eat healthy, drink lots of water, exercise
- Endless energy supply
- Exercise for a healthier future
- Exercise. It does a body good
- Experience yourself
- Extreme body makeover
- Feel the burn!
- Fitness connection
- Get things done
- Give it your all
- Hang in there
- Healthy trails to you
- High hopes
- Impossible mission
- In motion
- In step
- Intensity
- It starts here
- Just do it
- Just what the doctor ordered
- Let's see what you can do
- "Man" power
- Maximum fitness
- "Me" time
- Move forward
- No boundaries
- No stopping me now
- Nothing is impossible
- Peak performance
- Pursue perfection
- Set high standards
- Shape your body
- Shape your future
- Step by step
- Still standing
- Stomping grounds
- Strive for excellence
- Survival of the fittest
- Take one day at a time
- That had to hurt!
- The gym is my body shop
- Top notch
- Tuff stuff
- Unleash the power
- Warm up
- Yes, you can

EYES

(Font: Windsor Lt BT)

- Beauty is in the eye of the beholder
- Bright eyes
- Dreamy eyes
- Eye care for you
- Eyes of a child
- Favorite features
- For my eyes only
- For your eyes only
- His/her eyes, how they twinkle
- Oh, blue eyes
- Perfect vision
- Seeing eye to eye
- Sleepy eyes
- Soulful eyes
- The eyes have it
- The sun rises in your eyes
- Twilight eyes
- Vision of beauty
- 20/20 vision

Glasses

(Font: Square721 Ex BT)

- Eye can see clearly now
- Eye care for my eyes
- Eye care for you
- Eye eye doctor
- New focus
- Perfect vision
- "Son" glasses
- You look "spectac"ular
- 20/20 vision

Family

(Font: CAC Camelot)

A family is created with love
Adventures of the _____ family
All together
Anything's possible with family
Building our dreams
Calling all kids
Can't live without them
Celebrate the little moments
Cherish every moment
Child bearing
Circle of love
Comedy hour
Comfort zone
Comic relief
Cultivating tolerance and understanding
"Dear" crossing
Designed by (parents names)
Don't sweat the small stuff
Eight is enough
Enjoy the little things
Everyone needs their own spot
Families stick together
Family circle
Family feud/fiasco
Family first
Family for all seasons
Family fotos/photo-op
Family girl/guy
Family handyman
Family heirlooms
Family matters
Family ties/time
Family togetherness
Family-opoly
Fantastic four/five
Favorite family
Fearsome foursome/fivesome
Feeding frenzy
Find meaning in the little things
Focus on the family

Full/Fun house
Fun family photo-op
Game crazy
Getting together
Going places
Good conversation
Good housekeeping
"Heart"-chitecture
Homemade happiness
House of dreamers
I look up to you
I love being a parent
In good hands
Inseparable
Inspired by you
It's a family affair
Jolly good times
Kitchen conversations
Lap land
Lean on me
Let the games begin
Life in the fast lane
Life is nothing without family
Like no other
Listen up
Mad house
Made in America
May your lap always be full
Merry making
My family rocks
My golden ruler broke
My hero/heroine
My wife and kids
Nothing is impossible with family
Oh, so charming
On the loose
One at a time
One day at a time
Our crowd/house
Our offspring
Out of this world

25

Party in the park
Party of four/five
Penny for your thoughts
Plan B
Play more. Work less
Purely you
Real life heroes
Remarkable you
Room for one more
Safe harbor/haven
Safety net
Secret language/world of family
Some things never change
Spending our children's inheritance
Stranger than fiction
Sweet reunion
Taste of home
Terrific trio

The beauty of family
The incredibles
The next generation
Things that really matter
Three's company
True blue hero
Two/three girls and a guy
Two/three guys and a girl
Unconditional love
Unique talents
We are family
We came from _____
We came to stay
We did it!
What a pair!
What matters most
What's family without love?
Where the wild things grow
Wishing you well

Aunt

Auntie dotes
Auntie trust

Aunts 'R' Us
My aunt rocks

Brother

Band of Brothers
Between Brothers
My brother, my hero

My brother rocks
Oh brother, where art thou

Dad

A father's arms are a special place
A father's heart/lap is a special place
All tapped out
Coffee maker
Cordless dad, recharge with kisses
Daddies make everyday special
Dad in training
Dad rocks

Dad time
Dad-itude
Dad's love is endless/special
Dad's love is unconditional
Dad's love lasts forever
Dads 'R' Us
Dads rock
Dad's wallet is cash in a flash
Dad's wallet is cash land
Dear Dad
Father and child

Genuine American hero
Glad Dad
Glad you're my dad
Greatest American hero, my dad
Happy pappy
Happy you're my pappy
Hero worship
Honey-do list
How I met your mother
Life as a father

Mad dad
Make room for Dad
Mr. Mom
National Bank of Dad
Nursery man
Oh-oh, dad's mad
Rad/Super dad
The first man a little girl falls in love with, is her father
What's in your wallet?

Dadspeak

Be quiet
Because, that's why/I said so
Don't make me stop this car
Go to sleep!
Here. Do it this way
I don't care
I don't know
I love being a dad
I love you
I told you not to do that

Let's go fishin'
Let's go to a ball game
Listen up
No!
Settle down
Stop your fighting
Wait 'til your mother gets home
Wanna' go for a ride?
Wanna' watch the game?
Watch. I'll show you how

Daughter

Daddy's/Mommy's little sweetheart
Daddy's/Mommy's pride and joy
Farmer's daughter

Isn't she sweet!
Mom in training
The giggler
The little lady in our life

Grandchildren

Child of my child
Grandma's/Grandpa's little boy/guy
Grandma's/Grandpa's little girl
Grandma's/Grandpa's little playmate/pal
Grandma's/Grandpa's little sweetheart
Grandma's/Grandpa's pride and joy

Grandparents

A grandparent's love is endless/special
A grandparent's love is unconditional
A grandparent's love lasts forever
Generous grandmas/grannies/grandpa's
Genuine American hero
Genuine grandmas/grannies/grandpas
Golden girls/grannies/guys
Gorgeous grandmas/grannies
Grandma/Grandpa spoils us
Grandma is mom with extra frosting
Grandma, you're not fat. You're fluffy
Grandma's/Grandpa's hands
Grandma's/Grandpa's magic words
Grandparents 'R' Us
Great American hero
Great grannies
Hero worship
I look up to you
Playful papa
Sweet and sour
The journey to a grandchild's house is never ending
The journey to a grandchild's house takes forever

Mom

A mother like no other
A mother's arms are a special place
A mother's heart/lap is a special place
Before I was a mom
Being a mother
Chief cook and bottle washer
Cordless mom, recharge with kisses
Domestic goddess
Grocery getter
How I met your father
Life as a mother
Magnificent moms
"Mah"velous mom/mama
Mama makes music
Mama's family
Mischievous mom/mama
Mom in training
Mommies make every day special
Mommy dearest/time
Mommy-o Andretti
Mom's love is endless/special
Mom's love is unconditional
Mom's love lasts forever
Mom's moment
Moms 'R' Us
Moms rock
Mom's school bus
Mother knows best
Mother land
Multi-tasking mom
My mama didn't raise no fool
My mom, my hero
My mom rocks
Super mom
That's my mama
The mother of boys/girls has a special place in heaven
Working mom's lead a double life
You can't scare me. I'm a mom

Momspeak

Are you hungry?
Be nice
Be quiet
Because I said so
Because, that's why
Comb your hair
Did you wash behind your ears?
Do you have everything you need?
Don't fight
Don't forget your _____
Go to sleep!
I don't care
I love being a mom!
I love you
I told you not to do that
I'm cold. Put a sweater on.
No!
Put a clean shirt on
Settle down
Share with your brother/sister
That's nice/not nice
Time for bed
Wash your hands
Watch. I'll show you.
Wear clean underwear
You look nice
You want to do what?

Parents

A parent's love is endless/special
A parent's love is unconditional
A parent's love lasts forever
Coffee makers
Mastering the skill of parenting
Parental knowledge/wisdom
Parenthood is not for sissies
Parenthood - the toughest job you'll ever love
Parents are possessor's of knowledge
Parents are wise ones
Parents in training

Sister

My sister, my hero
My sister rocks
Sister, Sister
Sisterly love
Social sister
Soul sister

Son

Father in training
Fun son
Simply "son"sational
Soapy son
"Son" bathing
"Son" beam/day
"Son"kissed
"Son" room/spot
Sonny boy
Summer "son"
The little man in our life
Your smile is "son"shine

Fireworks

(Font: Pritchard Line Out LET)

Aim high
Create a storm
Delightful diversion
Do more
Fire in the night
Fire in the sky
Free Fallin'
High lights/hopes
Illuminations
In motion
Little firecracker
May your sparklers always light
Oooooohhh! Aaaaaahhh!
Savor the moment
Smokin' hot
Snap, crackle, pop
Somewhere in the night
We look up to you

Food

(Font: CAC Logo Alternate)

A filling experience
A real treat
Building blocks for a healthy future
Can't eat just one
Can't get enough
Can't live without it
Chow down/hounds
Comfort food
Dig in
Dinner is served
Everyday eating
Favorite foods
Feeding frenzy
Fill 'er up
Food fight!
Fun food
Give me something good to eat
Good eats
Have it your way
Healthy trails to you
Homemade happiness
Indulge in the things you truly love
Is it soup yet?
Jam session
Lip smackin' good
May your sandwich never get soggy
Open wide!
Savor the moment
Snap, crackle, pop
So much food, so little time
Some like it hot
Source of endless pleasure
Sweet stuff
Sweet tooth
Tantalizing tastes
Taste of home
Tempting, tasty treats
That'll tickle your taco
The ice cream is chilling
Tickles your tongue
Too much of a good thing
Try something new
Well seasoned

Baking

(Font: URWLinearTMed)

A filling experience
A real treat
Baker boy
Bread man
Cake maker
Chocolatier
Cookie crafter
Dough boy
Dough nut
Fun food
Good eats
Great gift
Ice man
Layer by layer
Lip smackin' good
Love to bake
Man/woman behind the oven
Oven lovin'
Pie man
Something so sweet
Step by step
Sticky fingers
Stuck together
Sweet greetings
Sweet smell of success
Sweet stuff
Sweet tooth
Tale of the sweet tooth

Cooking

(Font: Arial)

Betty Crocker, I'm not
Chief cook and bottle washer
Chocolatier
Claim to fame
Cooking for two
Cooking light
Crazy for cooking
Delightful diversion
Dinner is served
Do it yourself
Plays with matches
Doing your own thing
Express yourself
Fire man/woman
Get things done
Good ol' home cookin'
I suffer from OCD – obsessive cooking disorder
Kiss the cook
Light my fire
Looks like we made it
Love to cook
Makin' heat
Martha Stewart, I'm not
Mastering the skill of cooking
New found ability
Nobody does it better
Pleasant pursuit
Rachel Ray, I'm not
Ring of fire
Smokin' hot
Something's burnin'
Sticky fingers
Sweet smell of success

Grilling

(Font: Flamme LET)

A fire in the night
Backyard living
Barbecue babes/boys
Burn baby, burn
Burnt offerings
Claim to fame
Do it best
Don't torch the porch
Eat, drink, grill, eat, drink
Fire man/woman
Fire station
Get 'er done!
Give me something good to eat
God of the grill
Good eats
Good ol' home cookin'
Great balls of fire
Great grillin' girl/guy
Great grillin' grandma/grandpa
Grill daddy
Grill girl/guy
Grill god
Grill master
Have it your way
Krispy kritters
May your steaks always be sizzling
Nobody does it better
Pleasant pursuit
Savor the flavor
Smokin' hot
Some like it ho
Something's burning
Taste of home
Throw another steak on the grill
Trial by fire
Try something new
Tuff stuff
Well seasoned
What a grill master!
What's cookin', good lookin'

Friends

(Font: Arnold Boecklin)

A friend beyond compare
A friend's kindness
A friend's thoughtfulness
A tribute to _____
All together
Bosom buddies
Boy's club
Boys' noise
Can't live without them
Cherish every moment
Comedy hour
Comfort zone
Comic relief
Do more together
Dynamic duo
Eight is enough
Everlasting friendship
Family friends
Fantastic four/five
Favorite friends
Friends and neighbors
Friends from afar
Friends stick together
Getting together
Giggle fest
Giggling girls
Girls club
Girls on the loose
Girl's town
Girly girls
Going places
Good conversation
Good girls
Here's to friends
Here's to girlfriends
Hero worship
I look up to you
Inseparable
Inspired by you
It's a girl/guy thing
Jolly good times
Keys to friendship
Kitchen conversation
Life is nothing without friendship
Like family
Like no other
Made in America
May your friends always be fun
May your friends be many
Merry making
Most wanted
Near and dear friends
Neighborly neighbors
Nice neighbors
Noisy neighbors
Oh, so charming
On the loose
One at a time
Our crowd
Pal-ettes
Party of four/five
Penny for your thoughts
Play boys/girls
Play. It does a body good
Play more, work less
Purely you
Remarkable you
Remember me
Room for one more
Save haven
Safety net
Secret world of friends
Self-disclosure
Small town friends
So little time, so many friends
Some things never change
Sometimes you feel like a nut
Soul sister
Stranger than fiction
The adventures of _____
The beauty of friendship
The boy/girl next door

The good old boys
The incredibles
The jokers
The lively bunch
The odd couple
The party's over
The secret language of friends
The wonder of friends
They came from _____
They came to stay
Things that really matter
Three's a crowd
Three's company
To tell the truth
Tons of fun
Two girls and a guy
Two guys and a girl

Unconditional love
We did it!
We're outta' here
We've got a secret
We've got personality
What a pair
What I like about you
What matters most
What's happening?
When in doubt, call a friend
Where friends meet
Where the wild ones are
Wishing you well
Wonder of friends
Won't you be my neighbor
You touch my heart
You want to do what?
You've got a friend in me

Frogs

(Font: CAC Valiant)

A boy and his frog
At the hop, hop, hop
At the water's edge
Back to nature
Backyard living
By the big blue water
Communing with nature
Creature features
Custom sound
Designed by God
Designed by Mother Nature
Don't touch the frog
Frog catcher
Frog friendly
Frog legs, anyone?
Frog tales

Frog, the fly hunter
Froggy days
Frogs are fly catchers
God's wonders
How frogs catch bugs
How to catch frogs
Into the wild
Like no other
Little frog man
Mother Nature's wonders
Nature's best
Oh, what a frog
On the wild side
Our big backyard
Plays in puddles
Remarkable reptile

Ribbit, ribbit
Small wonder
Stranger than fiction
Tree frog
Unique talents
Urban frog
Watch for warts!

Watching wildlife
What frogs do
Where the wild ones are
Wild thing
Woods and waters
You've got the cutest little
    froggy face

Gambling

(Font: Tango BT)

A hard day's play
All bets are off
Ante up
Anything is possible
Can't get enough
Cha-ching
Deal me in
Delightful diversion
Do it best
Do your own thing
Eat, drink, gamble
Favorite pastime
Getting nothing for
    something
Hidden treasure
High hopes
High roller
Hooked on gambling
I believe in magic

Just do it!
Land of the lost
Las Vegas = lost wages
Mastering the skill of
    winning
May your jackpot always
    be large
Miss/Ms. Lucky
Mr./Mrs. Lucky
Nothing is impossible
Play on
Pleasant pursuit
Poker face
Spin to win
Strictly slots
Treasure hunt
Winners make things
    happen
You too, can be a winner

Gardening

(Font: Freefrm721 BT)

A rose between two thorns
Appreciating nature
Backyard living
Beautiful blooms of spring
Beautiful bougainvillea
Bloomin' beauty
Breath of fresh air
Bumper crop
Bushwhacking
Can't live without it
Claim to fame
Communing with nature
Country gardens
Country moments
Country side of life
Create tomorrow by what you dream today
Creative gardens
Dainty daisies
Delightful diversion
Designed by _____
Dig it
Dig right in
Dirt therapy
Dirty duds
Do it yourself
Do your own thing
Everything has beauty
Favorite pastime
Flowers are God's wonders
Flowers are little miracles from God
Flowers are Mother Nature's wonders
Flowers are my favorite things
Flowers make a landscape beautiful
Gardening is cheaper than a psychiatrist
Gardens aren't made by sittin' in the shade
Get out there
Get things done
Gigantic garden
Glorious garden/gardeners
Glorious gardenias
Glorious morning glories
Grand garden/gardeners
Great garden/gardeners
Great/grand gardenias
Great/grand morning glories
Green house gardener
Green house guy/girl
Green land
Green thumb gardener
Green thumb guy/girl
Grounds work
Growing like a weed
Growing pains
Growing up
Growth spurt
Happiness is digging in the dirt
Have it your way
Hearty hostas
Hoe, hoe, hoe
Homemade happiness

How does your garden grow?
I am a perennial gardener
I dig my garden
I do not have a green thumb
In good hands
Indulge in the things you truly love
Into the wild
It's a different world
Keys to success
Land scape
Like no other
Little seedlings
Lovely lilies
Luxurious lilies
May your posies always be perky
"Me" time
Mud therapy
Muddy duds
Mums the word
My beautiful garden
My garden is a little glimpse of heaven
My secret garden
My world and welcome to it
Natural splendors
Nature's beauty
Nature's best
New beginnings
New found ability
Nobody does it better

Peaceful pastime
Pleasant pursuit
Pocket full of posies
Pretty pansies
Pretty petunias
Pretty posies
Promise of life
Proof of Heaven's existence
Rambling roses
Regal roses
See weed
Seedin' and weedin'
Showered with love
Small wonder
Smallville
So many flowers, so little time
So many weeds, so little time
Source of endless pleasure
Spring clean up
Spring cleaning
The good earth
The magic garden
There is magic in everything
Tons of colorful tulips
Tulips to treasure
Water garden
Weed farm
Weed man
What's a little dirt?
Where the wild things grow
When in doubt, dig in dirt
Wonder of life

Growing older

(Font: HandelGothic BT)

A senior moment
AARP – all about rowdy people
Age doesn't matter
Do things you think you cannot
Don't count years – count memories
Eventful eighties
Fabulous forties/fifties
Fantastic forties/fifties
Fun forties/fifties
Golden oldies
Have it your way
Heaven can wait
I'm confused – wait – maybe I'm not
Indulge in the things you truly love
It's the pits
Looks like we made it
Making the most of now
Nimble nineties
Old age is no place for sissies
Older, but wiser
Older, but no wiser
Oldies, but goodies
Ornery octogenarian
Outgoing octogenarian
Sexy sixties/seventies
So life has a hill. Get over it.
Spending our children's inheritance
Stands out in a crowd
Still standing
Sweet and sour
The big cheese
The lively bunch
Think young
Thy heating pad and thy pain pills, they comfort me
Time keeps ticking away
Trying something new
Tuff stuff
Well seasoned
With age comes value
With age comes wisdom
Wrinkles show where smiles hang out
You're never too old to play
Youth is wasted on the young

Hair

(Font: CAC Pinafore)

Bubbles and shines
Bumper crop
Call of the wild
Cutting the curls
Designed by _____
Hair flair
Hair raising
Hair's how
Head liners
Hilarious hair
Historic hair
Huge hair
Humongous hair
Humorous hair
Let it shine
Location is everything
Mane event
May your hair always be there
The big bangs
The head quarters
Tons of tangles
Tough tangles
Wash and wear hair

Happiness

(Font: Script12 BT)

Can't live without it
Celebrate the little things
Don't leave home without it
Enjoy the simple things
Happily ever after
Happiness begins within
Happiness is _____
Happiness is a choice
Happiness is digging in the dirt
Happiness is dirt
Happiness is handmade
Happiness is meant to be shared
Happy hour
Homemade happiness
I'm in heaven
Jolly good times
Keep happy thoughts
Live on the happy side of life
Merry making
Sitting on top of the world
The key to happiness

Hats

(Font: Aurora BdCn BT)

A man/woman with hat-itude
Baby's bonnet is a baby hood
Brother hood
Child hood
Dat hat
Designed by _____
Fat hat
Father hood
Hat hair
High hats
Hilarious hats
Hooked on hats
Huge hats
Humorous hats
In style
Mother hood
Parent hood
Sister hood
Slip, slidin' away

Heritage

[Font: Old Towne No. 536]

_____ years revisited
A little bit of history
American history
Blast from the past
Favorite memories of _____
Good old days
Hands of time
History makers
If I could turn back time
If I knew then what I know now
If walls could talk
Lost in the forties/fifties/sixties
Memories of old
Memories of yesteryear
MVP - Most Valuable Photo
Old stomping grounds
Old time photos
Oldies but goodies
Once upon a time
Piece of history
Reminiscences
Roaring 20's
Stories of Christmas past
Sweet reunion
That was then, this is now
The early years
The evolution of _____
The old days
The old neighborhood
Timeless treasures
Times gone by
Turn back the hands of time
What were we thinking?
Yesterday

Hobbies

(Font: Exotc350 Lt BT)

_____ diva
_____ enthusiast
_____ pro
A hard day's play
American __(hobby)__
Art from the heart
Artistic hands
Awesome accomplishments
Be original
Break away from the ordinary
Busy body
Can't get enough
Can't live without them
Claim to fame
Constructive developments
Crafting craze
Crazy for crafting/creating
Create it
Creation station
Creative _____
Creative corner/craze
Creative outlet
Delightful diversions
Designed by _____
Discovering one's self
Do it best
Do it yourself
Do more
Do your own thing
Eat, drink, create
Enjoy the simple things
Excellent craftsmanship
Favorite pastime
Gift maker
Handcrafted elegance
Have it your way
Hobbies are cheaper than a psychiatrist
Hobby heaven
Homemade happiness
Hooked on _____
Ideas ahead
Imagination stirs the soul
Indulge in the things you love
Leave your mark
Looks like I made it
Mastering the skill of _____
"Me" time
Meet the artist
New found abilities
Nobody does it better
One thing at a time
Peaceful pastimes
Play more. Work less
Pleasant pursuits
Pursuit of perfection
So many hobbies, so little time
Source of endless pleasure
Step by step
Think outside the box
True calling Try something new
When in doubt, craft
Yes, you can!
You want to do what?

Needle crafts

(Font: Ignatius LET)

Classic stitcher
It's sew beautiful
It's sew good
It's sew much fun
May your needle always be sharp
May your stitches always be straight
Sew and sew

Sew many patterns, sew little time
Sew many stitches
Sewing savvy
Stitch wizard
Textile world
Timeless stitches
You sew sew well

Cross stitch

Counting the night away
Crazy for cross stitch
Cross-eyed stitcher
Extreme patience

required
Make every stitch count
The count/countess

Quilting

A love of quilting
Crazy for quilting
Crazy quilter
Quietly quilting

Quilt maker
Quilter's block
Quilting savvy
Quirky quilter

Photography

(FONT: CAESAR OPEN)

- AIM HIGH
- CAMERA CRAZY
- CAPTURES ENDLESS MEMORIES/MOMENTS
- CAPTURING A MOMENT IN TIME
- CAPTURING THE LIGHT
- CHALLENGE EVERYTHING
- DARK ROOM
- EVERYTHING HAS BEAUTY
- EXTREME CLOSE-UP
- FINDING THE MEANING IN EVERYTHING
- FRAME WORK
- FREEZING A MOMENT IN TIME
- IT'S A DIFFERENT WORLD
- LOCATION, LOCATION, LOCATION
- MASTERING THE SKILL OF PHOTOGRAPHY
- MAY YOUR BATTERIES ALWAYS BE CHARGED
- MVP ~ MOST VALUABLE PHOTO
- NATURE PHOTOGRAPHY
- PERSONALITY PORTRAIT
- PHOTO OP
- PHOTOGRAPHERS SUFFER FROM FLASH BACK
- PHOTOGRAPHY IS AN ART
- PICTURES DON'T LIE
- PORTRAITS OF LIFE
- PRECIOUS PORTRAITS
- RECORDING MEMORIES/ MOMENTS
- SAVE THE MEMORY/ MOMENT

Scrapbooking

(FONT: Exotc350 It BT)

- A crop/scrap above
- Album of memories
- Amazing keepsake creations
- Book keeper
- Book maker
- Cloth, paper, scissors
- Crazy for cropping/scrapping
- Crop/scrap away
- Crop/scrap for fun
- Crop/scrap for keeps
- Crop/scrap happy
- Crop/scrap it
- Crop/scrap lady
- Crop/scrap life
- Crop/scrap master
- Crop/scrap with style
- Crop/scrap yourself silly
- Cropper/scrapper extraordinaire
- Cropper's/scrapper's block
- Cropper's/scrapper's delight
- Cropping/Scrapping fool
- Cutting up
- Don't worry, be scrappy
- Dream book
- Dream keepers
- Flashbacks
- For keeps sake
- Forever cropping/scrapping
- Frame work

Gotta' crop/scrap
Happy cropping/scrapping
Have to crop/scrap
I suffer from OCD - obsessive cropping disorder
I'm croppin'/scrappin'
It's about time
I've caught the cropping/scrapping bug
Keepsake creations
Let's crop/scrap
Mad cropper/scrapper
May your scissors always stay sharp
Memory keeper
Nap time — scrap time
Paper magic
Paper trail
Phi Beta Croppa/Scrappa
Photographs to memories
Pictures to pages
PMS — Purchase More Scrapbooks/Supplies
Runs with decorative scissors
Save the memory
Save the moment
Scrapbook nook
Scrapbook station
Scrapbook therapy
Scrapbooker's anonymous
Scrapbookers stick together
Scrapbooking is a sticky subject
Scrapbooks are works of heart
Scrappin' sisters
Scrapping moments
Scrapping obsession
Scrapping on my mind
Scrapping sentiments
Scrap-ology
Scrap-tastic
Sensational scrapping
Sentimental scrapping
Snap and scrap
So many pictures, so little time
Something to scrap about
Sticker fingers
Sticky fingers
What's scrapbooking without memories?

Stained Glass

(Font: Odessa LET)

Cutting up
Foiled again!
Glass girl/guy
Glass guru
Gotta' have gloves
Memories in glass
Pictures in glass
Solder gun fun
Solder savvy

Stamping

Font: Verdana)

A stamp above
A stamper's life
Amazing keepsake
 creations
For keeps sake
Forever stamping
Gotta' stamp
Have to stamp
I have stamper's block
I stamp for fun
I'm a stampin' fool
I'm stamp happy
I'm stampin'
I've caught the stamping
 bug
Just stamp it
Let's stamp
Mad stamper
May your ink pad never dry
 up
Paper magic
Paper trail
Phi Beta Stampa
PMS - Purchase More

Stamps/Supplies
Sensational stamping
Sentimental stamping
Something to stamp about
Stamp away
Stamp for keeps
Stamp lady
Stamp master
Stamp therapy
Stamp with style
Stamp yourself silly
Stamp-aholic
Stamper extraordinaire
Stamper's anonymous
Stamper's delight
Stampin' sisters
Stamping moments
Stamping nook/station
Stamping obsession
Stamping on my mind
Stamping sentiments
Stamp-ology
Stamp-tastic
When in doubt, stamp

Woodworking

(Font: PO52L)

All about wood
Designed by _____
Excellent craftsmanship
Frame work
Half bubble off level
Hammer head
Handy man
I came, I sawed, I fixed it
If I had a hammer
Level headed

May your wood never
 warp
Nuts and bolts
On the level
Tool king/skills
Tools for success
Wood work
Woodworkers are on the
 level
Woodworker's block

Holidays

(Font: FormalScrp421 BT)

All together
Big plans
Celebrate the little moments
Cherish each moment
Cherish the little moments
Enjoy the simple things
Favorite time of year
Getting together
Give me something good to eat
Good eats
Good news!
Holidays celebrate each other
Holidays celebrate family
Holidays celebrate togetherness
My favorite holiday
Picture perfect holiday
Savor the moment
Seize the day
Taste of home
The big day
Things that really matter

Christmas

(Font: Brush 455 BT)

All I want for Christmas
All things bright and beautiful
Believe in magic
Christmas is family
Christmas kids
Christmas lights hung with love
Christmas through your eyes
Crazy for Christmas
Early Christmas morning
Find peace within
Glad tidings
Good golly, he's jolly!
Good golly, it's holly!
Hidden treasures
His eyes, how they twinkle
Hope and faith
I believe in magic
I'll be home for Christmas
Jolly follies
Jolly good times
Joys of Christmas
Joyous occasions
Klaus-trophobia
Little drummer boy
Magic town
May your tinsel always twinkle/never tangle
Merry Christmas baby
Merry makers/making
Mistletoe kisses/magic
Norman Rockwell holiday

Ornamentation
Pass the presents
Santa – an American legend
Santa baby
Santa Claus, I'm not
Santa has a jelly belly
Santa's apprentice/trainee
Santa's surprise
Scents of Christmas
Sense of wonder
Simply Santa
Sounds of Christmas
Stories of Christmas past/present
Thank you, Santa!
There is magic in everything
T'was the flight before Christmas
Up on the housetop/rooftop
What's Christmas without family/friends?
What's Christmas without kids?
When you believe
You're all I want for Christmas

Easter

(Font: Blippo BLK BT)

At the hop, hop, hop
Believe in magic
Egg-spressions
Find peace within
Hope and faith
I believe in magic
Joyous occasions
May your baskets always be full
May your jelly beans never get stale
Thank you, Easter Bunny!
The Easter Bunny I'm not
There is magic in everything
Treasure hunt
What's Easter without the bunny?
Where's that egg?

Halloween

(AmericanText BT)

A real treat
All dressed up, and nowhere to go
Bag of bones
Bare Bones
Bewitched
Blood donors needed
Bugs and hisses
Devilishly good looking
Entertainment tonight
Fearfully/frightfully fun
Ferociously/frighteningly fun
Ghastly greetings
Ghostly greetings
I vant to bite your candy/neck
I will spook when spookin' to
May your treats be sweet
Mini-monsters
Saturday night femur
Skeleton crew
So many houses, so little time
Somewhere in the night
Spectacular spooks
Sticky fingers
The great pumpkin
What's Halloween without candy?

Thanksgiving

(Font: Jillian gothic)

A filling experience
Bounty of blessings
Can't get enough
Chow down
Dig in
Dinner is served
Eat, drink, sleep
Feeding frenzy
Give me something good to eat
Gobble 'til you wobble
Gobblin' the turkey
Good eats
Lip smackin' good
Tantalizing tastes
Taste of home
Thanksgiving is family
Together again thankfully
Turkey tradition
What's Thanksgiving without turkey?

Home

(Font: Freehand591 BT)

_____ street blues
A home like no other
A town like no other
American home
Backyard camping/vacation
Backyard living
Coastal living
Comfort of home
Comfort zone
Country life/living
Dark room
Dream home
Empty nest
Green land
Heirloom home
Heritage home
Hidden corners
Hide away
High maintenance
Homemade happiness
House Beautiful
House of dreamers
House of many people
House of many rooms
Kitchen conversations
Little people's place
Log home living
Martha Stewart I'm not
Mother land
Mountain living
Open house
Our cozy kitchen
Our house
Our light house
Safe harbor/haven
Small town life/living
Stomping grounds
Taste of home
The old neighborhood
Things that really matter
Urban life/living
We came to stay
What matters most
What's home without love?
Where the wild things grow

Home Maintenance

Busy body
Constructive developments
Dirty duds
Do it right
Do it yourself
Do more
Do things you think you cannot
Extreme home makeover
Fence me in
Fresh coat of paint

Get things done
House coat
Just do it
No tools required?
Nobody does it better
Nothing's impossible
Renovation sensation
So many repairs, so little energy
Stir up some paint
Tuff stuff
Weekend warriors
What's a little dirt?
Wired
Work together as one
Yes, you can

Housework

Busy body
Chief cook and bottle washer
Clean pro
Clean sweep
Get things done
Good housekeeping
Housekeeping is homework
Iron work
Just do it
Nobody does it better
Spring cleaning
What's a little dirt?

New Home

Aim high
An amazing/awesome accomplishment
Anything's possible
Believe in the power of your dreams
Big plans
Break away from the ordinary
Do it yourself
Don't sweat the small stuff
Exceed your dreams
Getting things done
Having it our way
High hopes
Location, location, location
Never give up your dreams
Nobody does it better
Nothing's impossible
One day at a time
Open house
Realize the power of your dreams
Set high standards
Strive for excellence
Think outside the box
Thousands of possibilities await us
Trying something new

We had a dream, and it came true
We're so proud

Work together as one
Yes, we can
You asked for it!

Buying a home

Finding home
Finding our dream home

Home search
The price is right

New home construction

Bringing down the old house
Building our dream
Constructive developments
Designed by _____
Heart-chitecture

Home wasn't built in a day
House raising
The house that _____ built
The house that we built

Yard Work

Bushwhacking
Dig right in
Fence me in
Grounds work
Hedge hog
Lawn care by _____
Lawnmower man
Mow man

Muddy duds
Our big backyard
Ready to mow
Spring clean up
Tree trimming
Weed farm/man
Yard man

Hugs

(Font: VAGRounded BT)

A hug a day keeps the tears away
Bear hug
Can't live without them
Co-mingling
Eat, drink, hug

Huggable, lovable you
King/Queen of cuddle
May your hugs always be handy
When you're not here, my hug has a hole in it

INSPIRATION

(FONT: BREMEN BD BT)

(YOUR NAME) WISDOM
AIM HIGH
ALWAYS BE YOUR BEST
ANYTHING'S POSSIBLE
BE A LEADER
BE CONFIDENT
BE PERSISTENT
BE THE BEST YOU CAN BE
BE TRUE TO YOURSELF
BELIEVE IN MAGIC
BELIEVE IN THE POWER OF YOUR DREAMS
BREAK AWAY FROM THE ORDINARY
CELEBRATE THE LITTLE MOMENTS
CHALLENGE EVERYTHING
CHASE YOUR DREAMS, YOU MAY CATCH ONE
CHERISH EVERY MOMENT
CHERISH THE LITTLE MOMENTS
CONQUERING THE FEAR OF _____
CREATE A STORM
CREATE TOMORROW BY WHAT YOU DREAM TODAY
DETERMINATION
DO IT BEST
DO IT RIGHT
DO MORE
DON'T LOOK BACK
DON'T QUIT

DREAM BIG
DREAM WEAVER
DREAMS WARM THE HEART
EAT, DRINK, INSPIRE
ENJOY EVERYDAY MOMENTS
ENJOY EVERYDAY THINGS
ENJOY THE SIMPLE THINGS
ESCAPE FROM THE ORDINARY
EVERY PATH HAS A PUDDLE
EVERYTHING HAS BEAUTY
EXCEED YOUR DREAMS
EXPERIENCE YOURSELF
FIND MEANING IN THE LITTLE THINGS
FIND PEACE WITHIN
GET OUT THERE
GET THINGS DONE
GIVE IT YOUR ALL
GRAB LIFE BY THE TAIL
HANG IN THERE
HAVE IT YOUR WAY
HELP SOMEONE HELP ONES SELF
HIGH HOPES
HOPE AND FAITH
I BELIEVE IN MAGIC
I BELIEVE IN ME
IMAGINATION STIRS THE SOUL
INDULGE IN THE THINGS YOU TRULY LOVE
INSPIRED BY YOU
IT'S A GREAT DAY TO BE

ALIVE
JUST DO IT
KEEP HAPPY THOUGHTS
KEYS TO SUCCESS
LEAD THE WAY
LEAVE YOUR MARK
LIVE LIFE
LISTEN TO YOUR HEART
LOVE WHO YOU ARE
LOVE YOURSELF
MAKE A DIFFERENCE
MAKE THE MOST OF NOW
MAKE YOURSELF HEARD
MAY THE SUN SHINE WARM
   UPON YOUR FACE
MAY YOUR PASSION NEVER
   WANE
MAY YOUR SPIRITS SOAR
   TO THE SKY
MOVE FORWARD
NEVER FORGET YOUR
   WORTH
NEVER GIVE UP YOUR
   DREAMS
NOBODY DOES IT BETTER
NO ONE IS BETTER AT BEING
   YOURSELF THAN YOU
NOTHING IS IMPOSSIBLE
PLAY HARD
PLAY MORE, WORK LESS
PURSUE PERFECTION
REALIZE THE POWER OF
   YOUR DREAMS
SAVOR THE MOMENT
SEIZE THE DAY
SET HIGH STANDARDS
SHAPE YOUR FUTURE
STAND OUT IN A CROWD
STRIVE FOR EXCELLENCE
SURROUND YOURSELF
   WITH WHOM YOU LOVE
TAKE ONE DAY AT A TIME
THERE ARE NO
   IMPOSSIBILITIES
THERE IS MAGIC IN
   EVERYTHING
THINK AHEAD. STAY
   AHEAD
THINK OUTSIDE THE BOX
THOUSANDS OF
   POSSIBILITIES AWAIT
   YOU
TRY SOMETHING NEW
WINNERS MAKE THINGS
   HAPPEN
WORK TOGETHER AS ONE
YES, YOU CAN
YOU ARE MY INSPIRATION
YOU ARE MY ROLE MODEL
YOU'RE NEVER TOO OLD TO
   PLAY
YOU'RE WORTH IT

Kids

(Font: CAC Krazy Legs Bold)

_(#)_ simple rules for raising kids
A child's delight
A child's love is priceless
A Child's love - the most valuable thing on earth
A little glimpse of heaven
A parents wisdom
ABC: A Bright Child
All about me/you
Almost all grown up
An angel from the start
Ankle biter
Aren't I/you cute?
Baby sitter: $12; movie: $10; your sanity: priceless
Be happy I'm not a twin
Beautiful brace face
Believing in magic
Beyond expectations
Blank expressions
Boo boo's happen
Born to be loved
Chatterbox
Child of God
Child of my heart
Childhood wisdom
Children learn how to live/love/smile from their parents
Chow hound
Clueless
Complete angels
Cool kids
Custom sound
Cute character
Cutting the curls
Daddy's/Mommy's lucky charms
Dad's/Mom's little treasures
Devilishly good looking
Eight is enough
Everyone needs their own spot
Fantastic four/five
First born
Give me something good to eat
God's little miracles
Good Behavior
Good day, sunshine
Growing like a weed
Growing Pains
Growing up me/you
Growth spurt
Handle with care
Here comes trouble
Hero worship
He's/she's bewitching
He's/she's captivating/charming
High maintenance
Home grown
House of dreamers
I don't want to miss a thing
I look up to you
In a heartbeat
In good hands
Inseparable
It happens every day
It's a mystery
It's all about you
I've got a secret

I've got personality
Jam session
Keep learning
Kids are fringe benefits
Kitchen conversations
Lap land
Like no other
Listen up
Little people/seedling
Little people's place
Made in America
Magnifi-kid
Mild child
Miracles from God
Most wanted
Mother and child
My special angel
My world, and welcome to it
Nature's best
No greater joy
No one is better at being you, than you
Oh so charming
Our offspring
Our silver lining
Our sweet little valentine
Papa's pride
Parent in training
Party of four/five
Penny for your thoughts
Proof of Heaven's existence
Purely you
Raising dad/mom
Remarkable you
Sad sack
Small wonder
So blessed to have you
Someone sweet
Stands out in a crowd

Step by step
Sticky Fingers
Still standing
Stranger than fiction
Sweet and sour
Sweet smiles/stuff
Sweet young thing
Tale of the tooth
Tons of tangles
Tears happen
Tender/terrific tots
The Big Day
The Comeback Kid
The eyes of a child
The incredibles
The joy a child brings
The next generation
They came to stay
Things that really matter
Thousands of possibilities await you
To tell the truth
Touched by an angel
What a cutie!
What a little flirt!
What a pair!
What a sweetheart/sweetie!
What I like about you
What matters most
What not to wear
While you were sleeping
Yes, Dear
You fill my life with smiles
You ought to be in pictures
You touch my heart
Young Americans
Young ones
"You"niquely you

Your kisses and your hugs,
    they comfort me
You're grrreat!

You're worth it!
Youth today
You've got personality

Bath Time

All washed up
At the water's edge
Bare necessities
Bath and body works
Bathtub blues
Bubble babes/boys
Bubble, bubble, toil and
    trouble
Bubbles and shines
Good clean fun
Honey, I shrunk the kids
In hot water

Indoor pool
Slip, slidin' away
Slippery when wet
Soap
Soapy siblings/sons
"Son" bathing
Squeaky clean
Suds city
The Bathtub Gang
The naked truth
Water sports
Water works
Wet behind the ears

Boys

Ain't he sweet!
Backyard/barnyard boys
Bad boys, bad boys
Bosom Buddies
Boy's club
Boy's noise
Bug boy
Built boy tough
Busy boy
Clever boy/guy
Dad in training
High boy
It's a guy thing
Keep him safe
King of the carpet

King of the hill/sidewalk/yard
Little drummer boy
Little man
Man in training
Milk man
Mr. big time
Mr. lucky
Play boy
Prince of the park
Pure boy
Small town boy
Super boy/hero/human
Super little man
Sweet little boy
Tee ball king

The boy in the mirror
The boy next door
The boy with something extra
The kid's flipped his lid
The little man in our life
The little man who changed
   our lives
The secret language of boys

Toy boy
Toys of a boy
Two/Three guys and a dream
Two/Three guys and a girl
Watch over him
What's a boy without dirt/noise?
Wild man

Child's play

(child's name) in charge
A hard day's play
Action heroes
Adventures of _____
Anything's possible
Artistic hands
Arts and activities/crafts
Backyard living
Batman fan
Big plans
Breath of fresh air
Bringing down the house
Busy body
Carousel kid
Carpet cruisin'
Chasing dreams
Childhood pleasures
Claim to fame
Come outside and play
Comedy hour
Comic collector's corporate office
Comic relief
Complete savages
Computer kid
Constructive developments
Creation station
Creative kids

CSE: crime scene evidence
Curious ___(name)___
Curious minds
Curtain climber
Custom home builder
Dangerous age
Dare devil
Daytime drama
Deer crossing
Delightful diversions
Devil on wheels
Do you have ants in your pants?
Doing it yourself
Doing your own thing
Doll house diva
Don't fence me in
Dynamic duo
Endless energy supply
Food fight
Fort night
Future American Idol
Future four wheeler/fighter/
   fisherman
Game crazy
Go outside and play
Going places
He Man fan

57

Hide away
Homemade happiness
How to catch bugs
How to do everything at once
In motion
In search of .....
I've been hosed!
Jolly good times
Junior achievement
Just do it!
Karate kid
Kid's creative corner
Kid's rock
Kung Fu fighting
Kung Fu kid
Leader of the pack
Let's see what you can do
Little firecracker/sport
Little swingers
Lost in the laundry
Look what I made!
Madhouse
Merry making
Mission impossible
Mud therapy
Muddy duds
My little creation/creators
No stopping me now
Noise and toys
On the loose
One at a time
Our big back yard
Pee Wee Picasso
Play is children's work
Play. It does a body good
Play on
Play station
Playing, playing, playing
Plays in puddles

Plump pockets
Raising the roof
Real kids, Real Adventures
Rock around the clock
Romper room
Ruler of the Roost
Running Wild
Secret world of children
Seek and destroy
Shazam!
Smallville
So many kids, so little aspirin
Some things never change
Sometimes you feel like a nut
Spiderman/superman fan
Stomping grounds
Super hero
Tee ball expert/tot
Terrific toys
That dangerous age
That had to hurt!
The Comeback Kid
The incredibles
The lively bunch
The music scene
The party's over
The pretender
The sidewalk is my runway
Three's a crowd
Three's company
Time to move
Toddle time
Tons of fun
Tornado tot
Tot time
Tot town/toys
Towering tree house
Toy house/tycoon
Treasured teddy

Trying something new
Tuff stuff
Two/three boys and a girl
Two/three girls and a boy
Unique talents
We cannot have too large a
    party
What's a kid without noise?
What's a little dirt?
What's happening?
Where are the children/kids?
Where the wild things are

Whiz kids
Will wonder's never cease!
Wild cat
Wild child
Wired
Work together as one
Yes, you can
You and your big ideas
You want to do what?
Young riders
You're antsy
You're the boss

Girls

Ain't she sweet!
American girl
Barnyard babes
Clever girl
Giggle fest
Giggling girl
Girls are giggles with freckles
Girls club/town
Girls on the loose
Girl's rock
Girls twirl
Girly girls
Good girls
It's a girl thing
Keep her safe
Lady in training
Little lady
Milk maid
Miss big time
Miss lucky
Mom in training
My little woman

Princess of the park
Pure girl
Queen of the carpet
Queen of the sidewalk/yard/
    hill
Small town girl
Sweet little girl
Sweet thing
Super little girl/woman
Tee ball queen
The girl in the mirror
The girl next door
The girl with something extra
The kid's flipped her lid
The little lady in our life
The little lady who changed
    our lives
The secret language of girls
The wonder of girls
Three girls and a boy/dream
Two girls and a dream
Watch over her

59

Kids and babies

But he/she doesn't do
    anything except cry!
Can I feed him/her?
Can I help?
Can I hold him/her?
Can I play with him/her?
Can't he/she be quiet?
How long is he/she gonna live here?
I love him/her
No, it's my baby!
When can I play with him/her?
When's he/she gonna be old enough to play?
Why does he/she cry all the time?

Kids and pets

Can I have a puppy/kitty?
I'll clean up after it
I'll feed it
I'll play with it
I'll take care of it
I'll take him/her outside
Look what I found!
Yea, I promise

Kids on pregnancy

Can I feel it move, mommy?
How does it get out?
I'm gonna' have a brother/sister!
It's in Mommy's tummy
When's it gonna be here?

Kidspeak

But I don't want to
But I want to
But Mom/Dad
Can _____ come out and play?
Can I have a do-over?
Can I help?
Can I, huh? Can I?
Can I play?
Choose me!
Dad can. Why can't I?
Do I have to?
Ha ha. Do it again daddy/mommy
He did it
He hit me
He's pickin' on me

I already did it
I can do it
I can't wait
I did it!
I didn't do it
I double dog dare you
I don't know
I don't want to
I gotta' go potty
I gotta' pee
I will, I promise
I won't hurt him/her
I'll be careful
I'll show you how
I'm cold/hungry
I'm not cold/hungry
I'm not tired
I'm tired
It wasn't me
Leave me alone
Mom, he's/she's lookin' at me
Mom, he's/she's touching me

No-no's not my name
Thanks, Mom/Dad (this one isn't heard nearly often enough)
The dog did it
Uh, Uh!
Watch me, dad/mom!
We did it!
What do you wanna do?
Who, Me?
Why?
Why can't I?
You don't know how.
    You're just a baby
You said I could
You're adopted
You're mean!
You're not my brother/sister/boss!
You're not the boss of me
When?

<u>Nap time</u>

All tuckered out
Boy cot
Can I have a drink of water?
Catnap
Delightful dreams
Down time
Dozer
Dream catcher
Dream happy, little one
Dream maker/weaver
Dream on
Dreamscapes
Go to sleep my darling

Kid napper
Kiddy winks
Land of nod
May your bed always be cuddly
May your sheets always be soft
Nap sack
Night visions
Quiet moments
Sleeping Beauty
Sleeping the night away
Sleepy eyes/head

61

Sleepy/slumber time
"Son" down/rise
Sounds of silence
Tales from the crib
The best part of waking up

The napster
There's a monster under my bed
While you were sleeping

Potty training

Celebrate the little things
Doo your own thing
Eat, drink, poop, pee
Every path has a puddle
It's my potty and I'll try if I want to
Junior achievement
Just doo it
One day at a time

Poop deck
Pot luck
Potty hottie
Potty tales
Pretty little training pants
Prince/princess of the potty
Tot pot
Yes, you can!

Twins

Double the pleasure
Dynamic duo
Inseparable
They play well together

Too much of a good thing
"Twin"-nocence
Twice in a lifetime
What a pair!

kite flying

(font: uncial)

aim high
air craft
air ride
delightful diversion
do your own thing
flight training
fly guy
fly paper
flying so high
free fallin'
gliding light
high hopes
i look up to you
in motion
mastering the skill of flying
new found ability
peaceful pastime
pleasant pursuit
source of endless pleasure
what goes up...
what's a kite without wind?
wild blue yonder
wind dancer

Laughter

(Font: Zennor LET)

A laugh a day keeps the blues away
Can't get enough
Can't live without it
Comedy central/club
Comedy hour
Comic relief
Custom sound
Delightful diversion
Express yourself
For your amusement
Giggle fest
Giggling girls
Girls are giggles with freckles
Homemade happiness
Just what the doctor ordered
Laugh in
Laugh out loud
Laugh so hard your face hurts
Laughter — an instant vacation
Laughter - Don't leave home without it
Laughter is cheaper than a psychiatrist
Lively laughter
Lovely laughter
Make yourself heard
Source of endless pleasure

Life

(Font: Cheltenhm BT)

A life altering experience
A tribute to _____
A year in the life of _____
An American epic/tale
Backyard living
Beauty of life
Best year of my life
Boating life
Can't live without it/you
Casual life/living
Celebrate life
Children learn how to live from their parents
City life/living
Coastal life/living
Come on, let's live a little
Country life/living
Country side of life
Dedicated to life
Energize your life
Enjoying everyday life
Experience life
Facts of life
Family life
Grab life by the tail
I'll light up your life
Improving lives
Independent living
It's a great life
Leisurely living
Life as a parent
Life at it's best
Life before/after kids
Life behind bars
Life connections
Life cycles/lessons
Life goes on

Life history of _____
Life is an amazing adventure
Life is good
Life is nothing without _____
Life is nothing without family/friendship
Life is short. Enjoy every moment
Life's gifts are priceless/sweet
Lifestyles of the poor and obscure
Lifestyles of the rich and famous
Lifestyles of the rushed and stressed
Live a little
Live for today
Live life to it's fullest
Live on the happy side of life
Live your life
Log home living
Make life better
Marriage begins a new life
Married life
May your life be long and happy
Mountain life/living
My life's work
Once in a lifetime
Opportunity of a lifetime
Ordinary people, extra-ordinary lives
Outdoor life/living
Portraits/promise of life
Real life heroes
Saves lives
Savor life's small delights
Secret life of _____
Sexiest man/woman alive
Simplify your life

Small town life/living
So life has a hill. Get over it!
Take life one day at a time
That's life
The best things in life aren't things
The Double life of (your name)
The drive/ride of your life
The facts of life
The game of your/my life
The girl/guy who changed my life
The good life
The little lady/man who changed my life
What does the future have in store?
What to do with the rest of my life
What's life without someone to share it?
Wheel life
Wonder of life
The little man/woman in our lives
The love of my life
The man/woman in my life
The man/woman who changed my life
The simple life
There's more to life than increasing it's speed
Tide of life
Time of your life
Touching lives
Urban life/living
We're life long friends
Working for a living
Working moms lead a double life
You bet your life
You fill my life with smiles
You light up my life
You make life worth living/ wonderful/worthwhile
Your partner for life

Love

(Font: CAC Champagne)

A diamond is forever
A glance, a smile, a touch
A loving heart
Ain't he/she sweet
American Idol
Bear Hug
Beauty and the best
Bewitched
Beyond expectations
Born to be loved
Building our dreams
Cant get enough
Can't live without it
Captivated
Charmed
Cherish each moment
Choco-love
Comfort zone
Co-mingle
Dear crossing

Dream maker/weaver
Dreamy eyes
Dynamic duo
Everybody loves _____
Finding love
Found love/someone
Getting together
Good day, sunshine
Handle with care
Head over heals
Heart attack
Heart-chitecture
Help the ones you love
Hero worship
Hey girl/guy
Hold on to this moment
Hot property
How I met _____
I dream of _____
I love my man/woman
If I could save time in a bottle
In a heartbeat
Inseparable
Intensity
Key to love
King/Queen of cuddle
Kisses are messengers of love
LOL - Lots/Loads Of love
Let there be love
Lets talk about love
Like no other
Lip smackin' good!
Listen to your heart

Lost in love
Love always/blossoms
Love American style
Love is eternal/limitless/magic
Love is the best medicine
Love lifts me up
Love makes the world go 'round
Love notes/story
Love sick/spell
Love that lasts
Love - world's greatest mystery
Lover's lane
Maybe this time
Million dollar man/woman
Mission impossible
Modern marvels
Most wanted
Mr./Mrs. Romance/
    Romantic
Ms./Miss Romance/romantic
Obey the heart
Oh, so charming
One man woman
One woman man
Out of this world
Peace, love, and understanding
Perfect love/catch
Perfect moments
Portraits of Love
Right from the heart
Romeo and Juliet
Season of love
Second chances

Second time around
Secret world of love
Self disclosure
Showered with love
So in love
Something so right/sweet
Source of endless pleasure
Stick together
Summer romance
Super man/woman
Sweet emotions/greetings
Sweet reunion/stuff
Teach love by loving
The art of falling in love
The courtship of _____'s
   father/mother
The heart of the matter
The incredibles
The right one

The sexiest man/woman alive
The tide/way of love
Things that really matter
Three's a crowd
Time to move on
To _____ with love
Together again
Treasures form the heart
Treat her like a lady
Twilight eyes
Unconditional love
Vacation romance
Vision of love
What a find/pair!
What a sweetheart!
What love is all about
What matters most
Wonder of love

Lover's spats

(Font: Van Dijk LET)

A man and his car/boat –
   err wife
Baby it's cold inside
How's that workin' for ya'
If looks could kill

I'm in the doghouse now
What's love without a few
   disagreements?
Yes, Dear

Loving you

(Font: Amazone BT)

Ain't no sunshine when you're gone
All about us
Baby, you look/smell soooo good
Blue over you
Can't smile without you
Celebrating our love
Celebrating the day you brightened my world
Celebrating the person you are
Come away with me
Crazy for you
Drooling over you
For my/your eyes only
For your love
Forget me not
From me to you
Huggable, lovable you
I belong to you
I dream of you
I had a dream, and you came true
I look up to you
I will always be there
I love all that you do
I'll be true to you
I'll be waiting for you
I'll light up your life
I'm with you always
Inspired by you
It's all about you
It's so nice to be with you
It's you I love
Just as long as I have you
Lets fall in love
Losing sleep over you
Mad about you
Mastering the art of loving you
My beautiful/handsome valentine
My beloved
My favorite place to be is next to you
My heart beats for you
My heart murmurs to you
My heart smiles when I see you
My lady loves me
My love for you will never die
My perfect match
My silver lining

My special angel
My super hero
My sweet valentine
Oh, baby!
Only the best for you
Our love grows deeper every day
Penny for your thoughts
Purely/remarkable you
So blessed to have you
Sweet thoughts of you
Thank God I found you
The man/woman who changed my life
The one I love
The sun rises in your eyes
The way you love me
Then came you
This one's for you
Together we are one forever
Together we can do anything
We were made for each other
What I love about you
Whatever souls are made of, ours are the same
When you're not here, my hug has a hole in it
Will you still love me tomorrow?
With each kiss goes a part of my heart
Working together as one
Yes, Dear
You are my inspiration/rock
You are my role model
You are so beautiful to me
You are the center of my universe
You are the reason
You fill my life with smiles
You hold my heart
You light up my life
You make everything beautiful
You make life wonderful
You make life wort living
You make life worthwhile
You make me happy
You touch my heart
You'll always be my baby
You-nique
You-niquely you

Your kisses and your
    hugs, they comfort me
Your partner for life
You're all I ever
    wanted
You're all I need
You're bewitching
You're captivating/
charming
You're great
You're my everything
You're one of a kind
You're the one
You're worth it
You've got personality

Marriage
(Font: CAC Lasko Even Weight)

A diamond is forever
A perfect match
Beyond expectations
Big plans
Building our dreams
Can't live without you
Celebrating our love
Celebrating the day you
    brightened my world
Dynamic duo
Empty nest
For ever after
Homemade happiness
Hot property
In the heat of the night
Life before/after kids
Marriage begins a new life
Marriage begins a new world
Married life
Looks like we made it
Mr./Mrs. lucky
Mr./Mrs. romance
My husband/wife and kids
My husband, my hero
The man/woman in my life
The party's over
The secret language of lovers
Till the end of time
Together we are one forever
Tuff stuff
Two souls undivided
Work together as one
Yes, Dear
You belong to me

Weddings

(Font: Wedding text BT)

American bride
An aisle of smiles
Anything's possible
Beautiful bride
Blessed beginnings
Breathtaking bride
Building our dreams
Cherish every moment
Cosmo bride
Dynamic duo
Floating on air
For ever after
Getting together
Great groom
Great news!
Have it our way
High hopes
Hitching post
Honeymooners
Listen to your heart
New beginnings
One cannot have too large a party
Our perfect wedding
Savor the moment
Seize the moment
The big day
'Till death us do part
To love, honor, and cherish
Together as one
We believe in happily ever after
We believe in magic
We had a dream, and it came true
We take the cake
Western weddings are western unions
Wishing you well

Memories

(Font: Caslon540 BT)

A day we love to remember
Another year of memories
Anytime memories
Beautiful memories
Beautiful moments
Blast from the past
Captured memories/moments
Don't count years, count memories
Endless memories/moments
Endearing memories/moments
Enduring memories/moments
Favorite memories of _____
For ever after
Forever memories
Got memories?
Great times, great memories
Handmade memories/moments
Hands of time
Heartfelt memories/moments
Hold on to this moment
Homemade happiness
Homemade memories/moments
I carry your memory with me always
I carry your memory with me wherever I go
Lasting memories
Mad for memories
Magical memories
May all your memories be sweet
Memories are a source of endless pleasure
Memories are keepsakes
Memories are made of this
Memories are my favorite possessions
Memories galore
Memories in the making
Memories of old
Memories of yesteryear
Memories that really matter
Memories to treasure
Moments that warm my heart
Moments to remember
Mountain of memories
Musical memories
MVP – Most valuable picture
My memories will keep you alive in my heart
Now and again
Ordinary events, extra-ordinary memories
Pleasant memories/moments
Precious moments
Remember me
Reminiscences
Savor the memory/moment
Slip, slidin' away
Something to remember
Time to make another memory
Times gone by
Treasury of memories
Yesterday

MEN

(FONT: INFORMAL 011 BT)

A MAN AND HIS DREAM
A MAN LIKE NO OTHER
A MAN WITH HAT-ITUDE
A SPECIAL MAN
ACCORDING TO _____
AMERICAN MALE/MAN
ANYTHING'S POSSIBLE
BACHELOR FATHER
BAD BOYS, BAD BOYS
BAR THERAPY
BIG PLANS
BIG TOY TYCOON
BORN TO BE LOVED
BORN TO LEAD
BOSOM BUDDIES
BOYS AT HEART
BOY'S CLUB
BUILT TOUGH
BUSY BODY
CAPTIVATING
CHARMING
CHOW DOWN/HOUND
CLAIM TO FAME
CLEVER GUY
COFFEE MAKER
COMEDY HOUR
COMIC RELIEF
COMPLETE SAVAGES
CREATING A STORM
DEAR CROSSING
DEVIL ON WHEELS
DEVILISHLY GOOD LOOKING
DO IT RIGHT
DO MORE
DO YOUR OWN THING
EAT, DRINK, EAT, DRINK, EAT, DRINK.....
EAT, DRINK, GET FULL AND DRUNK
EXCEED YOUR DREAMS
FANTASTIC FOUR/FIVE
FAST ACTION HERO
GAME CRAZY
GETTING THINGS DONE
GIVE ME SOMETHING GOOD TO EAT
GOD OF THE GRILL
GOING PLACES
GRILL GOD/MASTER
GUITAR MAN
HANDSOME HUNK
HE-MAN
HE'S A LEADER
HE'S THE REAL THING
HISTORY MAKER
HOW'S THAT WORKIN' FOR YA?
I LOOK UP TO YOU
IN SEARCH OF....
IN THE HEAT OF THE NIGHT
IN YOUR WILDEST DREAMS
INTO THE WILD
IT'S A GUY THING
IT'S A MAN'S WORLD
JAVA TIME
JUST DO IT
KEYS TO SUCCESS
KING OF CUDDLE/DENIAL/ GOOD TIMES
KING OF WISHFUL THINKING
LADY'S MAN
LAND OF THE LOST
LAWN CARE BY _____
LAWNMOWER MAN
LEADING THE WAY
LESSONS LEARNED
LIFE BEFORE/AFTER KIDS
LIKE NO OTHER
LISTEN UP
"MAH"VELOUS MAN
MAKING A DIFFERENCE
MAN IN TRAINING
MAN OF INTEGRITY
MAN OF THE YEAR
MANLY MAN
MEN STICK TOGETHER
MEN'S TOYS ARE BIGGER THAN BOY'S TOYS
MERRY MUSIC MAN
MILLION DOLLAR MAN
MISCHIEVOUS MAN
MODERN GUY
MODERN MARVEL
MOST WANTED

MOVING FORWARD
MR. BIG TIME/LUCKY
MR. DREAMY/PERFECT
MUSCLE BOUND MAN
MY HANDSOME VALENTINE
MY WORLD AND WELCOME TO IT
NIGHT OWL
NO STOPPING ME NOW
NOBODY DOES IT BETTER
NOISE WITH BIG TOYS
NOT YOUR AVERAGE JOE
NOTHING IS IMPOSSIBLE
OH, SO CHARMING
ON THE LOOSE
ONE LADY AT A TIME
ONE WOMAN MAN
OUR CROWD
OUT OF SIGHT, OUT OF MIND
PARTY OF FOUR/FIVE
PAST ACTION HERO
PICTURES DON'T LIE
PLAN B
PLAY. IT DOES A BODY GOOD
PLAY MORE, WORK LESS
PURELY YOU
PURSUE PERFECTION
REALIZE THE POWER OF YOUR DREAMS
REMARKABLE YOU
REMEMBER ME
RULER OF THE ROOST
SAWING LOGS
SCRAPBOOK WIDOWER
SETTING HIGH STANDARDS
SIX MILLION DOLLAR MAN
SMOKIN' HOT
SO LITTLE TIME, SO MANY ____
SO LITTLE TIME, SO MANY DRINKS
SO MANY TOYS/WOMEN, SO LITTLE TIME
SOME THINGS NEVER CHANGE
SOME TIMES I FEEL LIKE A NUT
SOPHISTICATION
SOURCE OF ENDLESS PLEASURE
STANDING OUT IN A CROWD
STRANGER THAN FICTION
STRIVING FOR EXCELLENCE
SUPER HERO/HUMAN/MAN
TERRIFIC TOYS
THE EYES HAVE IT

THE GOOD OLD BOYS
THE GUY IN THE MIRROR
THE GUY WHO CHANGED MY LIFE
THE GUY WITH SOMETHING EXTRA
THE INCREDIBLE HUNK
THE INTIMIDATOR
THE JOKER
THE LIVELY BUNCH
THE MAN IN MY LIFE
THE SEXIEST MAN ALIVE
THE WONDER OF MEN
THIN MAN
THINK OUTSIDE THE BOX
THIS IS ME
THY RECLINER AND THY REMOTE, THEY COMFORT ME
TIME TO MOVE ON
TOO MUCH OF A GOOD THING
TOP DOG
TUFF STUFF
TWO/THREE GUYS AND A DREAM
TWO/THREE GUYS AND A GIRL
UNIQUE TALENTS
WANTED MAN
WANTED: MAN
WEED MAN
WE'RE NOT LOST
WE'RE OUTTA' HERE
WHAT A FLIRT!
WHAT NOT TO WEAR
WHAT TO DO WITH THE REST OF MY LIFE
WHAT'S A LITTLE DIRT?
WHAT'S IN YOUR WALLET
WHEN YOU'RE HOT, YOU'RE HOT
WHEN YOU'VE GOT IT, FLAUNT IT
WILL WONDER'S NEVER CEASE
WINNERS MAKE THINGS HAPPEN
WILD MAN
WIRED
YARD MAN
YOU AND YOUR BIG IDEAS
YOU ARE MY INSPIRATION
YOU ARE MY ROLE MODEL
YOU MIGHT BE A REDNECK IF..

YOU TOUCH MY HEART
YOU WANT TO DO WHAT?
YOU WISH!

YOU-NIQUE
YOU-NIQUELY YOU
YOU'VE GOT PERSONALITY

MEN AND HAIR

ANYTHING'S POSSIBLE
BALDYLOCKS
BUZZED
HAIR RAISING
HAIR TODAY, GONE
    TOMORROW

HIGH HOPES
LOCATION IS EVERYTHING
MAY YOUR HAIR ALWAYS
    BE THERE
OUT GROWTH
STRUGGLING HAIR FARMER

MEN AND TOOLS

DO IT BEST
DO IT RIGHT
DO IT YOURSELF
EAT, DRINK, FIX THINGS
EXTREME HOME MAKEOVER
FAVORITE TOYS
HAMMER HEAD
HANDY MAN
HOOKED ON TOOLS
IF I CAN'T FIX IT, IT AIN'T
    BROKE
IF I HAD A HAMMER

JACK OF ALL TRADES
JUST DO IT!
LEAVE YOUR MARK
MAN POWER
MORE POWER
NO TOOLS REQUIRED!
NOBODY DOES IT BETTER
NOTHING IS IMPOSSIBLE
PLEASANT PURSUIT
SOME ASSEMBLY REQUIRED
TOOL KING

Music

(Font: Staccato 222 BT)

Band-ettes
Battle of the bands
Can't live without it
Car tunes
Custom sound
Delightful diversion
Feel the beat
Golden oldies
Good tunes
Indulge in the things you love
Jazz time
Let the music move you
Magic of music
Magical/mystical music
Many moods of music

Music creates peace and harmony
Music is what feelings sound like
Music moves/stirs my soul
Music sets my soul on fire
Music to my ears
Musical memories
My favorite musician
Name that tune
Pleasant pursuit
Rockin' all night long
Solid gold
Sound waves
Source of endless pleasure

Music Makers

A different drummer
Band wagon
Be confident
Believe in the power of your dreams
Claim to fame
Create a storm
Do things you think you cannot
Do your best
Do your own thing

Drummer dude
Exceed your dreams
Fastest guitar alive
Fiddle stick
Future American Idol
Getting a tune up
Guitar guru/man
Homemade happiness
I write the songs
Jazz band
Keep on playing/singing

Little drummer boy
Mama makes music
Master of music
Merry music man
Mini Mozart
Mozart I'm not
Mr. music man
Music machine
Music makers/master
Musicians rock
My favorite musician
Never give up your dreams
New found ability
Nobody does it better
Nothing is impossible
Passion for the piano
Play music for me
Play on
Pursue perfection
Realize the power of your
    dreams
Set high standards
Set the night to music
Stand out in a crowd
Strive for excellence
The music scene
Thousands of possibilities
    await you
Travelin' band
True calling
When in doubt, make music
Yes, you can
You are my inspiration/role
    model

Nature

(Font: CAC Krazy Legs)

Adopt the pace of nature
Appreciate nature
Back to nature
Bear/Deer crossing
Beautiful one day, perfect the
    next
Best of the great outdoors
Beyond expectations
Breath of fresh air
Bushwhacking
Can't beat Mother Nature
Can't live without it
Communing with nature
Country side of life
Daybreak
Designed by Mother Nature
Falling water
Gentle country moments
Get out there
God's country
Green land
Hidden treasures
Incredible views
Into the wild
Intriguing trees
It's a different world
Listening to nature
Magnificent wilderness
Miracles from God
Mother nature's wonders

Natural splendors
Nature lover
Nature's beauty/best
Nutcracker
Our big back yard
Pure, natural, unspoiled
Rustic countryside
Scenic wonders
Seasons change
Serenity of the forest
Source of endless pleasure
Star gazing
Stranger than fiction
That's water under the bridge
The best of the great outdoors

The good earth
The promised land
Through our windows, nature entertains us
Uncharted territory
Walk with nature
Walks among nature
Watching wildlife
What a beautiful world
What's a little dirt?
Where the wild things are
Woodland wilderness/wonders
Woods and waters
Woods walk

Pets

(Font: AdLib BT)

A little glimpse of heaven
A passion for pets
A real treat
Adopt a pet
Ain't he/she sweet
All God's creatures/ critters
Angels among us
Angels on earth
Animal antics/circus/fair
Ankle biter
Amazing pets/pet stories
American made
Aren't I cute?
Back yard boys
Back yard life/living
Bad boys, bad boys
Barnyard critters
Bewitching
Beyond expectations
Born to be loved
Breaking away from the ordinary

Busy little body
Can't live without them
Captivating
Carpet cruisers
Charming
Chow down
Clever little thing
Comedy hour
Comic relief
Complete savages
Creating a storm
Creature comforts/ features
CSE: crime scene evidence
Custom sound
Cute little characters
Cute little critters/ creatures
Delightful diversions
Designed by God
Designed by Mother Nature

Don't fence me in!
Don't leave home without them
Dreamy eyes
Dynamic duo
Eight is enough
Endless energy supply
Family pet
Fantastic four/five
Favorite pets
Feeding frenzy
Finding home
First born
Four on the floor
Fur face
Give me something good to eat
Go outside and play
God's little miracles
Going places
Good behavior
Good boy/girl
Good old boys
Good things come in small packages
Grab life by the tail
Grazin' in the grass
Growing like a weed
Growth spurt
Handle with care
Heaven sent
Here's the scoop, pick up the poop
Hero worship
He's/she's here to stay
High maintenance
His/her eyes, how they twinkle
Home made
Homemade happiness
I don't want to miss a thing
In motion
Indulge your pets

I've got personality
Just what the doctor ordered
King/Queen of cuddle
King/Queen of the carpet
King/Queen of the yard
Land of the lost
Lap land
Leader of the pack
Leading the way
Leaving your mark
Let's go outside and play
Let's see what you can do
Life behind bars
Like no other
Love at first sigh
Mad house
Made in America
May your pet always be perky
Miracle from God
Most wanted
My world and welcome to it
Nature's best
Newcomer
No greater joy
No stopping me now
Oh so charming/sweet
On the loose
One at a time
Our big backyard
Perfect love
Perky pets
Pet property
Pets are cheaper than a psychiatrist
Play boy/girl
Play. It does a body good
Play on
Plump pets
Pretty pets
Promise of life

Proof of heaven's existence
Purely you
Raising the roof
Remarkable you
Rock climbing/crawling
Romper room
Room for one more
Ruler of the roost
Running Wild
Sad but true
Seek and destroy
Showered with love
Smallville
Small wonder
So little time, so many _____
Something so sweet
Source of endless pleasure
Stomping grounds
Stranger than fiction
Sweet stuff
Sweet thing
Tales of the teeth
Terrific toys
The eyes have it
The good earth
The house that _____ built
The incredibles
The lively bunch
The pitter patter of little feet
The real McCoy
The wonder years
They came to stay
Things that really matter
Things we learn from our pets
Tiny souls
Tons of fun
Treasured toy
Two/three/four/five/six of a kind
Unconditional love
Unique talents
Upwardly mobile pet
Urban pet
We came to stay
We're outta' here
What a cutie!
What a pair!
What a sweetheart/ sweetie!
What's a little dirt?
What's the worst that could happen?
When in doubt, pet your pet
Who needs a therapist? I have a _____
Who's he/she, and how long is he/she staying?
Wired
You ought to be in pictures
You touch my heart
Young ones
Young riders
You-nique
You-niquely you
Your petting and your voice, they comfort me
You're adorable/charming
You're worth it
You've got personality
You've got the cutest little _____ face

Birds

Air male
Air ride
Bird man
Bird observer/watcher
Cagey, aren't you
Cagey cockatoo
Custom home builders
Empty nest
Fine feathered friend
Flight training
Fly guy
I am birdie, hear me sing
I am birdie, watch me fly
I look up to you
Life behind bars
Little swinger
May your cage always be clean
Pretty parakeet/parrot
Ruler of the roost
Wind dancer

Cats

Alluring/amazing angora
Bless my whiskers
Calico cat
Cat and mouse
Cat call
Cat fancier
Cat kisses
Cat nip
Cat tail
Cat woman
Cats and dogs
Cats are miracles with tails
Cats crawl into our hearts
Cats – the only love money can buy
Cats up
Catsville
City/Country cat
Crazy for cats
Cuddly calico
Cuddly cat
Curiosity killed the cat
Desperate house cats
Don't touch the cat
Family cat
Fancy felines
Feline fever
Feline fun
Fun felines
Funny felines
Furry felines
I am kitty, hear me meow/roar
I am kitty, watch me play
Kitty capers/kisses
Kitty city
May your litter box always be clean
Meows massage the heart
Milk maid/man
Miss prissy
My cat can lick anyone
Purr-fect pair
Purr-fectly adorable
Pussy foot
Pussycat, pussycat
Sassy Siamese
The cat's meow
The red Cat Society
Urban cat

When in doubt, pet your
    cat
Wild cat
You're a cat!

Kittens

A brand new life
After birth
Calico kittens
Crazy for kittens
Cuddly/Curious kittens
Eight is enough
Free kittens are not free
I'm here!
Kitten call
Kitten capers
Kitten cuties
Kitten kisses
Kittens are so cute
Kittens crawl into our
    hearts
New beginnings
Sweet little seedling
Sweet young thing
Tail of two kittens
The next generation
We're here!
When in doubt, pet a
    kitten
When in doubt, play with
    a kitten
Wonder of life
You are here!
Young one
You've got the cutest
    little kitty face

Dogs

(Dog's name) the big/small
    (dog's color) dog
A dog lives to hear his/her
    master's voice
A man and his dog
Barking up the wrong tree
Bashful/beguiling beagle
Bless my whiskers
Bone appetit/jour
Charming/Comical collie
Chow hound
City dog
Country dawg
Cute little Chihuahua
Dawg byte
Delightful dachshund/dog
Dig in
Dog and kennel
Dog smarts/tales/trot
Dog, the bird hunter
Doggy days
Dogs are miracles with
    paws/tails
Dogs crawl into our
    hearts
Dogs – the only love
    money can buy
Dogs unleashed
Don't fence me in
Don't touch the dog
Drooling over you
Dynomutt
Eight is enough
Every dog should have a
    boy
Family/Guard dog
Fido friendly
Hot dog

Humongous hound dog
Humorous hound
I'm in the doghouse now
Joyful/jumpin' jack russell
Lap dog
Let sleeping dogs lie
Little Lhasa Apso
Loving/lovable lab
Muzzle loading
My dog can lick anyone
My dog is a muzzle loader.
    He fills his muzzle faster than a speeding bullet.
My favorite mutt
Oh, what a dog!
Our granddogs
Plays in puddles
Poodle puddle
Pretty poodle
Pug-nacious
Regal retriever
Roofer
Sensational shepherd/spaniel
Springy shepherd/spaniel
Tail of two dogs
Tales of the teeth!
Terrific terrier
That bark!
The Dogfather
The intimidator
The shaggy dog
Things we learn from our dogs
Top/Urban dog
What dogs do
When in doubt, pet your dog
Where sleeping dogs lie
Who let the dogs out?
Wonder dog
Woods walk
Your licks and your wags, they comfort me
You're a dog!
You've got the cutest little doggy face

Puppies

A brand new life
After birth
Bless my whiskers
Free puppies are not free
Hush puppy
I am puppy, hear me bark
I am puppy, watch me play
I'm here!
May your puppy always be playful
Perky/Playful puppies
Pitiful puppy
Plays in puddles
Pretty puppy
Puppies are miracles with paws/tails
Puppies crawl into our hearts
Puppies – the only love money can buy
Puppy dog tales
Puppy licks/play
Puppy school
Sweet little seedling
Sweet young thing
Tail of two puppies
The next generation
We're here

When in doubt, pet your
    puppy
When in doubt, play with
    your puppy
Wonder of life

You are here!
Young one
You've got the cutest
    little puppy face

Ferrets

Family ferret
Fancy ferret
Ferret fever
Ferret fun
Funny ferret
"Let"tuce eat

May your ferret always
    be furry
Salad bar
You've got the cutest
    little ferret face

Hamsters

Free wheeling
Gotta wheel
Hamster haven/heaven
Huggable hamster
"Let"tuce eat
Look at him/her fly!
May your wheel always
    be greased

Salad bar
The wheel of the hamster
    goes round and
    round
Wheel fanatic/fun
You've got the cutest
    little hamster face

Horses

Adventurous appaloosa
An "oat" meal
Classic Clydesdales
Creature comforts
Creature features
Filly buster
Filly fever/fun
Grazin' in the grass
Hitching post
Horse and rider
Horse man
Horse play/power
Just horsin' around

May your oats always be
    edible
May your saddle always
    be shiny
My pretty pony
Perfect Painted/palomino/
    pinto
Pony boy
Pony tales
Ponys are "quarter"
    horses
Pretty painted/palomino/
    pinto

Proud painted/palomino/
   pinto
Quick quarter horse

Sweet little Shetland
Young riders

Iguanas

Fly catcher
How to catch bugs
Incredible iguana
Laughable lizard
Lazy/Lucky lizard
"Let"tuce eat
Linoleum lizard

Lizard lover
May your lettuce never
   wilt
On the wild side
Remarkable reptile
Salad bar

Rabbits

Four on the floor
Funny bunnies
Fur face
Grazin' in the grass
"Let"tuce eat

Master of multiplication
May your carrots always
   be crisp
Rabbit factory
Salad bar

Snakes

Big Boa
Eatin' it whole!
Give me a little snaky lick
Remarkable reptile

Shedding your skin
Silly snake
Slippery/Slithery snakes
You snake!

Pregnancy

(Font: Pink LET)

A short nine months
A waiting game
Agony of the feet
All I want is you
A long 9 months
Beauty is in the eye of the beholder
Bigger isn't necessarily better
Building our dream
Cherish every moment
Constructive developments
Craves-a-lot
Eat, drink, pee
Experience yourself
Family planning
Feeling fat, fat, fat
Feeling frumpy
Getting bigger by the minute/moment
Going the distance
Hang in there
'Heart'chitecture
Here we go again
He's/she's a kicker
He's/she's a mover and a shaker
How much longer?
I can hardly breathe/move
I can't wait much longer
If I could turn back time
I'm craving _____
I'm in shape. Round is a shape
I'm preggers

It starts here
It's a girl thing
Life before kids
Make the most of now
Mission impossible
No pain, no gain
No turning back now
Nobody does it better
Nothing fits anymore
One at a time
One day at a time
One on the way
Parent in training
Promise of life
Queen of denial
Roller coaster of emotions
Room for one more
Second time around
Sweet little sensations
The long haul/wait
The main event
The name game
There's no stopping him/her now
This is no joke!
This kid's in motion 24/7
Twice in a lifetime
Ultrasound bound
Waiting, waiting, waiting
We've got a secret
Yes, you can
Young rider
You're glowing/growing

Professions

(Font: Lucida Console)

A lifetime of service
Aim high
Anything's possible
Be a leader
Be all you can be
Be confident
Be your best
Believe in the power
   of your dreams
Big plans
Born to lead
Built tough
Busy body
Career world
Chase your dreams
Claim to fame
Clever one
Constructive developments
Determination
Discovering one's self
Do it best/right
Do it yourself
Do more
Do your own thing
Don't quit
Eat, drink, work
Exceed your dreams
Get things done
Give it your all
Hang in there
History makers
I look up to you
It happens every day
Just do it
Keys to success
Lead the way
Leave your mark
Let the work begin
Life's work
Man/Woman behind the desk/
   uniform
Man/Woman of the year
Mastering the skill of
   _____
Mr/Mrs/Miss/Ms big time
Mission impossible
Modern marvels
Moonlighting
Move forward
Multi-tasking
My world and welcome to it
New found abilities
Night crew/owl
No stopping me now
Nobody does it better
Nothing is impossible

Occupational hazard
On the job
Opportunity of a lifetime
Opportunity's knocking
Our crowd
Plan B
Pursue perfection
Second chances
Set high standards
Shape your future
Skeleton crew
Some things never change
Strive for excellence
Super human
Survival of the fittest
Taskmaster
The apprentice/big cheese
The price is right
The real McCoy
There's opportunity here
Think ahead; stay ahead
Think outside the box
Thousands of possibilities
   await you
Time to move on
Tools for success
Top banana/dog
Top notch
Tough stuff
True calling
Unique talents
Vacation motivation
We do good work
We're outta' here!
What a great _____
   looks like
What not to wear
What to do with the rest
   of my life
What's in your wallet?
What's my line?
What's new for 2007?
When experience counts
Where information lives
Whistle while you work
Work with me
Workin' 9 to 5
Workin' for a living
Working moms lead a double
   life
Yes, you can
You and your big ideas
You are my role model
You want to do what?
Your ticket to the world
You're the boss

Accountant

(Font: Bookman Old Style)

Balancing the books
"Count"er intelligence
Figuratively speaking
Human calculator
It all adds up

Master of multiplication
Math man
Pencil pusher
The count

Astronomer

(Font: Orbit-B BT)

Aim high
Catch a falling star
Communing with nature
I look up to you
Incredible views
It's a different world
Land escape
Location, location, location
Man/woman behind the
   telescope
May your stars always be
   bright
May your stars always shine
Natural splendors
Night owl
Night Visions
Out of this world
So many stars, so little time
Somewhere in the night
Star hunter/gazer
Stars are high lights
Uncharted territory

CARPENTER

(Font: Arial Black)

All about wood
Builders/Carpenters are on
   the level
Builders/Carpenters are
   studs
Cat on a hot tin roof
Constructive developments
Custom home builder
Designed by _____
Excellent craftsmanship
Extreme home makeover
Frame work
Half bubble off level
Hammer head
Handy man

Heart-chitecture
Home maker
Home wasn't built in a day
House breaker
If I had a hammer
Level headed
Man/Woman behind the
   hammer
Master carpenter
No tools required?
Nuts and bolts
On the level
Raising the roof
Renovation sensation
The house that _____ built

These boots are made for
   workin'
Tool king
Tools for success

Transformers
Up on the rooftop
Wood work

Clock repairman

(Font: CAC One Seventy)

Clock work/wise
Eat, drink, fix it
Excellent craftsmanship
Keeping time
Man/woman behind the

workbench
Right on time
Tick tock
Watch what he's/she's doing

Computer Technician

(Font: Futura MD BT)

Computer corner
Computer genius/whiz/geek
Crazy for computers
High tech
I suffer from OCD – obsessive
   computer disorder

Mr. fix it
Proficient in programming
Repair guru
Tech time
Technically speaking
True techie

Dentist

(Font: Bauer Bodni BT)

DDS: Designs Delightful
   Smiles
Gentle dental
Improving health
King/Queen of the office
Life's work
Man/woman behind the
   needle/drill
Open wide

Renovation sensation
Say ahhhh
So many teeth, so little time
Tale of the tooth
Trading faces
Transformer
Working for a healthier
   community
X-ray expert

ELECTRICIAN

(FONT: LATIN XCN BT)

BUZZED
CONSTRUCTIVE DEVELOPMENTS
FISHIN' FOR WIRE
HIGH VOLTAGE
HOT STUFF
LINE MAN

SPARKY
UNDER THE LIGHTS
WIRED
YOU LIGHT UP MY LIFE
ZAPPED

Engineer

(Font: Lydian BT)

Designs darn near anything
Equations "R" US
Highly educated
Math man

Pencil pusher
Plan B
Plans ahead
Technically speaking

Exterminator

(Font: Smack LET.)

Bug man
Competing with nature
Don't bug me
Eat, drink, kill pests
Seek and destroy

So many pests, so little time
Termite terminator
The terminator
You're driving me buggy

Factory worker

Font: CAC Futura Casual Bold)

Agony of the feet
Assemblyman
I walk the line
Lineman

Nuts and bolts
Still standing
Stomping grounds
These boots are made for workin'

Farmer

(Font: Freehand 575 BT)

All God's creatures/critters
Animal antics
Animal circus/fair
Appreciates nature
Barnyard babe/boy
Barnyard big shot/boss
Barnyard creatures/critters
Barnyard life/living
Breath of fresh air
Bull pen/dozer
Bumper crop
Bushwhacker
Communing with nature
Country side of life
Cow boy
Dairy Air farmer
Dig in
Diggin' the dirt
Dirt therapy
Dirty duds
Don't fence me in

Feeding frenzy
Grazin' in the grass
Green acres/land/pastures
Grounds work
Hay day
Hog wash
I dig my farm
King/Queen of the fields
May all your fields be full
Mud therapy
Muddy duds
Planting produce
Plays in puddles
Praying for rain
Ruler of the roost
Rustic countryside
Stomping grounds
Successful farming
The good earth
These boots are made for workin'
Tuff stuff

Up at dawn
Up with the chickens

What's a little dirt/mud?
Young riders

Firefighter

(Font: Varga LET)

A fire in the night
Bucket brigade
Career world
Cat on a hot tin roof
Feel the burn
Hot bed
Hot blooded
In the heat of the night
Into the inferno
Life guard/saver

Night crew
No smoking
Saves lives
Smokin' hot
Snap, crackle, pop
Survival of the fittest
The great fire
Trial by fire
What's a little dirt?

Hairdresser

(Font: CAC Shoshone Brush)

Agony of the feet
Bad hair day
Bubbles and shines
Bushwhacker
Cutting corner
Cutting the curls
Hair farmer/razor
Hair flair/line
Hairdressers are transformers

Hair's how
Head hunters/liners
Head quarters
Man/woman behind the scissors
Mane event
Scissors palace
Shear expressions/madness
Shear paradise/pleasure
Still standing

Jeweler

(Font: Park Avenue BT)

Artistic hands
Designed by _____
Excellent craftsmanship
Genuine jeweler

Joy of jewelry
My jeweler is a gem
My jeweler is priceless
24 carat gold jeweler

Judge

(font: Libra BT)

"con" tester
defender of justice
in charge/control
just the facts
justice league
king/queen of the court

law man
man/woman behind the
    bench/robe/gavel
so many criminals,
    so few convictions
the intimidator

Laboratory technician

(Font: MisterEarl BT)

Biology babe/boy
Lab animal
Man/woman behind the
    scrubs/needle
Master of the microscope

Stomping grounds
Technically speaking
Test tube talent
Working for a healthier community

Lawyer

(Font: Zurich Lt BT)

Brief case
Just the facts
Law Man/suit
Law school lad/lass

Man/woman behind the
    briefcase
Passing the bar

Manager

(Font: Kis BT)

Between a rock and a hard place
Born to lead
Getting things done
In charge
Lead the way
Middle man
Moving forward
Set high standards
Task master
The big cheese
Top banana/dog
When experience counts
Work with me
You're the boss

Mechanic

(Font: Incised 901 Nd BT)

Auto restorer
Auto zone
Body shop boy
Body shop babe
Car tunes
Devil on wheels
Getting a tune up
Man and machine
Man over machine
Man/woman behind the overalls
Motor man
Nuts and bolts
So many cars, so little time
Stomping grounds
These boots are made for workin'
Tire tester
Tool king
Tools for success
What's a little grease?

Minister

(Font: Goudy OlSt BT)

At home with my faith
Christian life/living
Faith at work
For the love of God
Magnificent/Moving Minister
Man/woman of the cloth
Meaningful ministry
Ministers to others
Ministry man/woman
Miraculous minister/missionary
Missionary man/woman
Oh come all ye faithful
Pious pastor/preacher/priest
Prayer man/woman
Prays for parishioners
True calling
Words of faith

Nurse

(Font: CaslonOpnface BT)

Agony of the feet
Can't live without them
Dedicated to life
First class
Florence Nightingale/
    Clara Barton I'm not
Future Clara Barton/
    Florence Nightingale
Improving lives
Just what the doctor ordered
King/Queen of the corridors
Life guard
Life saver
Man/woman behind the
    bed pan/needle
Man/Woman behind the
    scrubs
Medicine Man/woman
Nursing is an art of the
    heart
Saturday night femur
Still standing
Stomping grounds
These shoes are made
    for walkin'
Touching lives
When experience counts
Working for a healthier
    community
X-ray expert

PAINTER

(FONT: ORLANDO LET)

Brush hog
Color coordinator
Fresh coat of paint
High maintenance
House coat
Man/woman behind the overalls/brush
Man/woman of many colors
Stir up some paint

Physician

(Font: CAC Leslie)

Cant live without them
Dedicated to life
Heart healer
Improving life
It's a miracle
Just what the doctor ordered
King/Queen of the office
Lab animal
Life guard/saver
Man/Woman behind the white coat/needle
Medic
Medicine man/woman
Open wide
Promise of life
Saturday night femur
Say ahhhhh
Stomping grounds
Survival of the fittest
Touching lives
Trading faces
Transformers
Working for a healthier community
X-ray expert

Pilot

(Font: Schadow BlkCn BT)

Air male/ride
All about airplanes
Defying gravity
Flight fanatic
Flight training
Fly-guy
High boy
I came, I saw, I went flying
I can fly
I look up to you
Into the wild blue yonder
King/Queen of the friendly skies
Land escape
Land of the lost
Location, location, location
Look at him/her fly
Man/Woman behind the propeller
Pilot prowess
Plane and pilot
Rocketeer
Sky king/pilot
The aviator
Uncharted territory
When in doubt, go flying

Police Officer

(Font: Challenge Extra Bold LET)

Bad boys, bad boys
Brief case
"Con" found
"Con" tend er
Cruise control
CSE: crime scene evidence
Defender of justice
In the jailhouse now
Just the facts
Justice league
Law Man/suit
Life's work
Man/Woman behind the gun/wheel
May your badge never tarnish
Motor man
Night crew
Prison blues
So many bad guys, so few police
Stomping grounds
Survival of the fittest
SWAT – Stunned With A Tazer
The intimidator
Thy gun and thy bullets, they comfort me
Tools for success
You're the boss

[SPEEDING TICKET #80]

Prison Guard

(Font: Futura XBlkCn BT)

A guard takes a "con" census
Bad boys, bad boys
"Con" tender
In the jailhouse now
Jailhouse blues
Justice league
Man/woman behind the badge
Night crew
Prison blues
Stomping grounds
The big house
The intimidator

Psychologist

(Font: Calligraph421 BT)

Dr. Phil I'm not
Heart healer
How's that workin' for ya'?
Improving life
Just what the doctor ordered
Life saver
Penny for your thoughts
Self disclosure
Touching lives
What's the worst that could happen?
Working for a healthier community

97

Secretary

(Font: Courier New)

Behind every success-
    ful boss is a
    great secretary
Computer king/queen
Indispensable
King/Queen of the
    office
May your computer
    never crash
May your pencils
    always stay sharp
Multi-tasker
    extraordinaire
Multi-tasking master/
    maven
Paper Chase
Paper/Pencil pusher

Store clerk

(Font: BernhardFashion BT)

Counter intelligence
Helps others
Man/Woman behind the
    counter
Ringing up the register
Still standing
Stomping grounds

Tattoo artist

(Font: OzHandicraft BT)

Artistic hands
Body art
Claim to fame
Create it
Creation station
Creative corner
Creative outlet
Creative tattooing
Designed by _____
Ink fever
King/Queen of ink
Man/Woman behind the needle
Master tattoo artist
Meet the artist

Teacher

(Font: CAC Lasko Condensed)

Cultivating tolerance and understanding
First class
May your ruler never break
My golden ruler broke
One good teacher outweighs a ton of books
Paper chase
Paper/Pencil pusher
Possessor of knowledge
So many students, so few teachers
Task master
Teachers inspire
Teachers open doors
The intimidator
The love of learning
Those that love, teach
Touching lives
Trials and tribulations of teaching
Wise one
You're the boss

Train engineer

(Font: Futura XblkCnIt BT)

American express
Coast to coast
Full speed ahead
I've been workin' on the railroad
Man and machine
Man/Woman behind the controls
Master hauler
Modern marvel
Moving forward
Riding the rails
Roll on
"Train"er
Where the journey begins/ends

Truck Driver

(Font: PosterBodoni It BT)

American express
Bumper to bumper
Business traveler
Coast to coast
Cruise control
Cruisin' in style
Devil on wheels
Down the road
Full speed ahead
Got wheels?

I'm getting there
I'm on my way
In search of....
I've come this far
King/Queen of the road
Land of the lost
Leave the driving to me
Location, location, location
Lonesome highways
Man and machine
Man/Woman behind the wheel
Master hauler
Miles to go before I sleep
Modern marvels
Motor man
Moving forward
My turn to drive
Passion for the open road
Pit stop
Roll on
Somewhere down the road
The call of the open road
The long road home
The streets of _____
Wheel life
Where the journey begins/ends
Where to go/stop
Zoom, zoom, zoom

Veterinarian

(Font: Scruff LET)

Animal circus/fair
Animal healer
Country side of life
Dedicated to the health of animals
Helping Nature's best
Medicine man/woman
Passion for pets
Pet pal/vet
Tales of the teeth
Where the wild things are

Waiter/Waitress

(Font: Commercial Script BT)

Agony of the feet
Tends tables
Host with the most
Hostest with the mostest
I'll wait for you
Sensational/super server
Servers "R" Us
Sophisticated/skillful server
These shoes are made for waitin'

Tip time
Wait for me!
Waiting the night away
Waits for work

Wise waiter/waitress
Wonderful waiter/waitress

Relaxation

(Font: Allegro BT)

Adopt the pace of nature
Backyard living
Beautiful one day, perfect the next
Can't get enough
Can't live without it
Casual living
Communing with nature
Do your own thing
Eat, drink, eat, drink
Enjoying everyday moments/things
Favorite pastime
Find peace within
Gentle country moments
Go outside and play
Have it your way
Homemade happiness
Indulge in the things you truly love
Jolly good times
Just what the doctor ordered
Lazy days
Leisurely living

Life is good
Merry making
Our big backyard
Peace and quiet
Peaceful pastime
Play. It does a body good
Play more. Work less
Pleasant pursuits
Relaxation anticipation
Savor the moment
Serene Saturday/Sunday
Simple Saturday/Sunday
Solitude is sweet
Sounds of silence
Sweet serenity
Take one day at a time
There's more to life than increasing it's speed
Through our windows, nature entertains us
Tons of fun
Walk with nature
When friends meet
Woodland wonders
You're never too old to play

School

(Font: Century Schoolbook SWA)

_____is in a class of her/his own
A + student
Absorbing everything
Aim high
Always do your best
An amazing mind
Assignment _____
Be a leader
Be all you can be
Be confident
Big boy/girl bus
Blackboard jungle
Brain work
Busy bodies
Chalk it up
Challenge everything
Clever boy/girl/guy
Concentration camp
Copy right
Crazy for crayons
Curious minds
Determination
Do it best
Do it right
Down by the schoolyard
Eat, drink, study
Exceed your dreams
Expand your mind
Fast/Fun times at (school name) High
Food fight
Forward thinking
Get things done
Getting great grades
Good behavior
Grade school big/hot shot
Guess work
Head quarters
High school big/hot shot
High school confidential
I don't have anything to wear
I love my school
Ideas ahead
It's a different world
It's all elementary
Juvenile Jungle
Keep learning
Kindergarten kid
Kindergarten roundup
King/Queen of the classroom/playground
Lessons learned
Let the work begin
Let's see what you can do
Look what I did/made!
Math man
Make a difference
Making the grade
Middle school big/hot shot
My world and welcome to it
New found abilities
Newcomer
No one left behind
No stopping me now
Nothing is impossible
On your best behavior
Paper chase
Paper/pencil pusher
Passport to adventure
Preschool prince/princess
Pursue perfection
Room for one more
Saved by the bell
School belles
School master/mistress
Set high standards
Shape your future
So much homework; so little time

Stomping grounds
Strive for excellence
The incredibles
The lively bunch
The love of learning
Think ahead; stay ahead
Think outside the box
Too cool for school
Tools for success
Try something new
Unique talents
Up grading to high school
What a great student looks like
What not to wear

What to wear
What's school without lunch/recess/sports?
When's lunch?
When's recess?
Where information lives
Where the wild things grow
Whiz kids
Wildlife management area
Yes, you can
Young ones
Young scholar
Your ticket to the world

College

(Font: Freefrm710 BT)

_____ goes to college
Big plans
Chase your dreams
Far, far away
Food fight
Getting great grades
In search of ....
Independent living
Keep learning
Leaving home
Letter from home
Looks like I made it
Math man
My world and welcome to it
Night owl
No stopping me now

On my own
On the loose
Opportunity of a lifetime
Opportunity's knocking
Shape your future
Strive for excellence
There's opportunity here
Up grading
What a great college student looks like
What to do with the rest of my life
Where information lives
Where the wild things are
Yes, you can!
Your ticket to the world

Graduation

(Font: Square721 Ex BT)

(# of grads) wise men/women
Big plans
Chase your dreams
Explore new frontiers
Going places
I'm free!!!
In search of....
In the working world
Independence day
Job search
Leaving home
Looks like I made it
No stopping me now
On my own
On the loose
Survivor
The big day
The future's bright
The great escape
Thousands of possibilities await you
Time to move on
We're outta' here!
What a great graduate looks like
What to do with the rest of my life
Wishing you well
Your ticket to the world

school dance

(Font: Fine Hand LET)

At the hop, hop, hop
Express yourself
Happy feet
I hope you dance
I look like a penguin!
In motion
In step
Just do it!
Lead the way
Let the music move you
Party line
Prom prep
Rockin' all night long
Save the last dance for me
Set the night to music
Shall we dance?
The lively bunch
The party's over

Seasons

(Font: Monotype Corsiva)

Appreciating nature
Beautiful one day, perfect the next
Beyond expectations
Breath of fresh air
Can't beat Mother Nature
Communing with nature
Designed by God
Designed by Mother Nature
Everything has beauty
For our entertainment
Get out there
God's wonders
Into the wild
Mother Nature's wonders
My favorite season
My favorite time of year
Nature at it's best
Nature's beauty
Seasons change
Source of endless pleasure
The great outdoors
Through our window, nature entertains us
Walk among nature
What a beautiful world

Fall

(Font: Hobo BT)

Autumn leaves are falling
Awesome autumn
Colors of fall, a vision for all
Cool, crisp days of autumn
Fall clean up
Fallen leaves
Free Fallin'
Grounds work
Rake, run, and roll
What's fall without color?

Font: Signet Roundhand)

Awakenings
Beautiful blooms of spring
Green land
Grounds work
New beginnings
Portraits of spring
Season of love
Spring clean up
Spring cleaning
Spring is nature's way of saying lets party
What's spring without flowers?

What's spring without rain?   *Wonder of life*

Summer

(Font DomCasual BT)

Beautiful one day, perfect the next
Big plans
Do your own thing
Good day, sunshine
Grounds work
Here's the scoop
Hot hut
Hot town in the summertime
Hydro massage
Hydrophobia
Hydrotherapy
In the heat of the night
Just chillin'
Just hangin' out
Lickin' the heat
Life at it's best
May the sun always shine
Outdoor life
Passport to adventure
Peaceful pastimes
Pleasant pursuits
Scoop it up
So long summer
Sounds of summer
Splash of color
Splashin' in the summer sun
Sprinkling of fun
Summer romance
Summer smiles
Summer sun
Summer's over
Summertime, and the livin' is easy
Sun city
Sun day
Sunbeams
Sunny boy
Sunshine
Tender foot
The good/sweet life
The ice cream was chilling!
What I did on my summer vacation
What's a little dirt
What's summer without a vacation?

At the pool

At the water's edge
Beating the heat
Cool blue water
Good clean fun
H2Ohhhhh
Hydrophobia
Hydrotherapy
Jewel of the pool
Lickin' the heat
Pooling our resources
   to build our pool

Slip, slidin away
Soak city
Splash of color
Splashin' in the summer sun
Summer splash
Swimsuit edition
The wonder of water
Too cool for the pool
Water world
Waterworks
We rule the pool

Sun tanning

A place in the sun
Burn baby, burn
Burnt offerings
Feel the burn
Feelin' hot, hot, hot
Fire station
Heating and cooling
Krispy kritters
Sand tanner
Sittin' in the summer sun
Soakin' up the sun

Some like it hot
Someone's burning
Sun dried
Sun guard
Sun kissed
Sun seekers
Swimsuit edition
Tanning lotion: BBQ sauce
   for the skin
Trial by fire
Working on my tan

Winter

(Font: Laser Chrome LET)

- A slow snow
- Arctic zone
- Auntie freeze
- Beauty of new fallen snow
- Blizzard blues
- Boots are "snow" shoes
- Closed for the season—reason—freezin'
- Cool headed
- Feeling cold, cold, cold
- Flakes are us
- Free snow, shovel all you want
- Free snowman, some assembly required
- Freezing family/friends
- Frigid air
- Frosty boy/girl
- Frosty family/friends
- Frozen assets
- Frozen buns
- Frozen family/friends
- Frozen toes
- It's a different world
- No snow
- Our place, on ice
- Shiver shack
- Slip, slidin' away
- Snow fall
- Snow goer
- Snow is angel's fairy dust
- Snow kidding
- Snow king/queen
- Snow memories
- Snow seekers
- Snow struck
- Snowbound
- Snowflakes are winter's butterflies
- So much/little snow
- Take time to chase the snowflakes
- The big chill
- The cold hard facts
- What's winter without snow?
- White is wonderful
- White wonder
- Warm up

Shopping

(Font: Parisian BT)

_____, my favorite place to shop
Agony of the feet
All tapped out
Can't get enough
Can't live without it
Cha-ching
Checkbook/Credit card/Money, don't leave home without it
Delightful diversion
Favorite pastime
Finding treasures
If the shoe fits, buy the matching purse
I've got nothing to wear
Moonlight madness
MVP — Most Valuable Purchase
No stopping me now!
PMS — purchase more stuff
Shopping in paradise
Shopping, shopping, shopping
So many stores, so little money
Source of endless pleasure
Spending our children's inheritance
Still standing
Treasure hunt
What a find!
What's in your wallet?
What's the point of window shopping?

SLEEP

(FONT: BREMEN BD BT)

ALL TUCKERED OUT
CATCHING SOME ZZZ'S
CATNAP
DARK ROOM
DELIGHTFUL DREAMS
DOWN FOR THE COUNT
DOWN TIME
DOZER
DREAM CATCHER
DREAM MAKER
DREAM WEAVER
DREAMSCAPES
GETTING A LITTLE SHUTEYE
HOUSE OF DREAMERS
LOSING SLEEP OVER YOU
NIGHT VISIONS
POWER NAP
QUIET MOMENTS
SAWING LOGS
SLEEPING BEAUTY
SLEEPING THE NIGHT AWAY
SLEEPY HEAD

SLIP, SLIDIN' INTO SLEEP
SLUMBER TIME
THE BEST PART OF WAKING
   UP

THINGS THAT GO BUMP
   IN THE NIGHT
WHILE YOU WERE SLEEPING

Smiles

(Font: Jokerman Let)

Can't get enough
Can't live without them
Can't smile without you
Children learn to smile from their parents
Comic relief
Don't leave home without them
Fastest smile in the west
Fastest smile in town
For your amusement
Homemade happiness
Keep smiling
May your smile always be bright
Our little boy's smiles are "son"beams
Our little boy's smiles are "son" shine
Put a smile on
Sensational smiles
Piles of smiles
Small smiles
Smile – it increases your face value
Smile – it makes people wonder what you're up to
Smile – it makes you look great
Smiles are contagious – be a carrier
Smiles that never fade
Source of endless pleasure
Super smiles
Sweet smiles
You fill my life with smiles
Your smile makes my heart flutter/jump
Your smile makes my heart sing

Sports

(Font: Century Gothic)

_(sport)___ action
_____ champs
_____ is life
_____ more, work less
_____ pro
_____ season
_____, the way it's meant
   to be played
_____ world
A fighting chance
A hard day's play
A sporting proposition
Adrenaline rush
Agony of the feet
Aim high
Always do your best
American athlete
American gladiators
An American legend
Anything's possible
Athlete's feet
Bad boys, bad boys
Battle of the _____
Be a leader
Be confident/fearless/proud
Be the best you can be
Beyond expectations
Big plans
Bone crusher
Born to lead/win
Born to play/perform
Brave heart
Break away from the ordinary
Bring it on!
Built tough
Busy bodies
Can I have a do-over?
Can't be beat
Can't get enough
Can't live without it
Challenge everything
Chase your dreams
Claim to fame
Close, but no cigar
Complete savages
Crazy for _____
Create a storm

Daredevil
Dedication
Delightful diversion
Determination
Discovering one's self
Do it better/best/right
Do not try this at home
Do things you think you cannot
Do your own thing
Don't quit
Endless energy supply
Exceed your dreams
Fast and the furious
Favorite pastime
Fear factor/nothing
Fearfully/Frighteningly/Frightfully
   fun
Future _____
Future pro
Game day
Gear up
Get out there
Get things done
Give it your all
Go outside and play
Going places
Greatest American hero
Grudge match
Hall of fame/shame
Hang in there
Hero worship
High hopes
History makers
I am invincible
I came , I saw, I conquered
I came , I saw, I got conquered
I look up to you
I'm out to win
In grand style
In motion
In your wildest dreams
Indulge in the things you truly
   love
Intensity
It starts here
Just do it!
Keys to success

King/Queen of the _____
King/Queen of wishful thinking
Lead the way
Leader of the pack
Leave your mark
Less talk, more walk
Less than perfect
Let's see what you can do
Lightning fast
Like no other
Little sport
Live out loud
Living on the edge
Madhouse
Make some noise
Man power
Mastering the skill of _____
Maximum velocity
May your passion never wane
Miss/Mr./Mrs./Ms. Big time
Miss/Mr./Mrs./Ms. Lucky
Mission impossible
Move forward
My pads and my cup, they comfort me
Never give up
New found abilities
No boundaries/nonsense
No stopping me now
Nobody does it better
Nothing is impossible
On the loose
One step ahead
Over the top
Passion to perform
Peak performance
Persistence
Pictures don't lie
Plan B
Play boy/girl
Play hard
Play. It does a body good
Play more; work less
Play on
Player of the year
Playing, playing, playing
Playing with dignity/power
Pleasant pursuits
Power play
Practice is the best teacher
Prime time sports

Pursue perfection
Ready, set, go
Run about
Sad but true
Score big
Second chances
Second time around
Seek and destroy
Set high standards
Shape your future
Simply the best
Sittin' on top of the world
Six million dollar man
Slip, slidin' away
Smokin' hot
So many games, so little time
Source of endless pleasure
Sports afield/illustrated
Sports are cheaper than a psychiatrist
Sports master/night
Stand clear
Stand out in a crowd
Still standing
Stomping grounds
Strive for excellence
Super boy/girl
Super hero/natural
Super human/man/woman
Super star status
Survival of the fittest
Sweet smell of success/victory
Take down
Takes a licking, but keeps on ticking
Tall tales
That had to hurt
The A-team
The agony of defeat
The best in the county/ state
The best in the school/world
The big day
The comeback kid
The defenders/master/rookie
The girl/guy with something extra
The heat is on
The incredibles/intimidator
The lively bunch
The road to victory
There's no stopping me now

They came from _____
Think ahead; stay ahead
Throw back
Time out
To play it safe, is to not play
Toast of the town
Tons of fun
Too much of a good thing
Tools for success
Top dog/notch
Tough man
True calling
True heroes earn respect
Tuff stuff
Ultimate adventure
Ultimate game/match
Ultimate fan/sports
Undefeated
Unique talents
Unleash the power
Unrivaled
Victory seekers
Warm up
We are the best
We can taste victory
We did it!
Weekend warriors

We're number one
We're outta' here
What I did on my summer vacation
What's a little dirt/mud/pain?
What's happening?
What's school without sports?
When you win, nothing hurts
When you're hot, you're hot
Will wonders never cease
Winners make things happen
Winner's way
Winning edge
Winning isn't everything
Winning with style
World class
World's best
X-treme _____
Yes, you can
You are my inspiration/role model
You can't win without trying
You wish
You're an all-star
You're grrreat!
You've got guts
You've got star quality

Auto Racing

Auto zone
Break pads
Breaking away
Burning rubber
Car and driver
Car craft
Custom machines
Devil on wheels
Fast finish
Faster than a speeding bullet
Faster than the speed of light
Four on the floor
Got wheels?
Helmet hair/head
High speed
Inside track
It's the pits
Look at him/her fly
Man and machine

Man over machine
Motor madness/mania
Motor man/woman
Nascar madness
Noise and toys
Pit stop
Race issues
Ride like the wind
Road and track
Road racers
Smokin' hot!
Speed demon/king/queen
Tearing up the tread
The amazing race
The drive of your life
Ticket to ride
Victory lane
Wheel life
Zoom, zoom, zoom

Boxing

- A fighting chance
- Bone crusher
- Box/Boxer boy
- Grudge match
- Knock out
- Man power
- May your gloves be golden
- Muscle man
- On the ropes
- Perfect match
- Pow wow
- Step by step
- Takes a licking, but keeps on ticking
- The big bang
- The comeback kid
- The intimidator

Fencing

- Don't fence me in
- Drat! Foiled again
- Good swordsmanship
- Light saber
- On the fence
- Sharpening your skills
- Sword play
- Sword sparring

Golf

- Birdie king/queen
- Birdie man/woman
- Bogie king/queen
- Bogie man/woman
- Course pro
- Different strokes
- Fairway fiasco
- Future Tiger Woods
- Game crazy
- Golf digest/illustrated
- GOLF of COURSE
- Golf quarterly/times
- Golf tips/world
- Golfing grannies/grandpas
- Grounds work
- Hole in 1--0
- Hole in one hopeful
- Keep your eye on the ball
- Nice shot
- 19th hole
- On the green
- Perfect match
- Praying for par
- Sand trap
- "Son" strokes
- Stroke smart
- Tee it up
- Teed/Teeing off
- Tiger Woods I'm not

Karate

- A fighting chance
- Block buster
- Faster than a speeding bullet
- Faster than the speed of light
- He takes a licking, but keeps on kicking
- It's a kick
- Kung Fu fighting/kid
- May your belt be black

Skateboarding

Air male/ride
Break pads
Break-neck-n'
Catchin' air
Defying gravity
Devil on wheels
Easy rider
First set of wheels
Flight training
Fly-guy
Foot loose
Free fallin'
Got wheels?
Head over heals
High boy
I came, I saw, I went skateboarding
I can fly
Look at him/her fly
Man over board
Perfect balance
Ride like the wind
Skateboarding prohibited: NOT!
Wheel man
When in doubt, go skateboarding
Young riders

Team Sports

Eat, drink, score
Game crazy/frenzy
Game day/plan
Game face/pro
Get your game on
Good game
Good luck at state
Got spirit
Greatest game ever played
Home team advantage
Hooray for our team
It's all in the game
It's how you play the game
Name of the game
Teaming up
The best in the league/school
The best in the county/state
The big/great game
Watching the big game
When in doubt, play _____
Winning team

Baseball

Angels in the outfield
Baseball bully
Bat man
Behind the bat
Curve ball
Dirty duds
Double/Triple play
Fast ball
Fly catchers
Helmet hair/head
High ball/fly
In the dugout
Keep your eye on the ball
May your bases always be loaded
Muddy duds
On deck
Pitching in
Play ball
Steeee-rike
Strike out
Tee ball boy/girl/tot
Tee ball king/queen
The perfect catch

115

Basketball

- Backboard bounce
- Basketball bully
- Basket maker/master
- Free throw
- Great save/shot
- He shoots, he scores!
- High ball/boy
- Hoops anyone?
- Jump shot
- May every shot swoosh
- Net work
- Nice/Open shot
- Sharp shooter
- Shootin' hoops
- Step by step
- Swoosh
- Winning at hoops

Bowling

- Bowling babes/boys
- Bowling ball bounce
- May all your pins fall
- Pin-ball game
- Spare king/queen
- Step by step
- Steeee-rike
- Sticky fingers
- Strike king/queen
- Strike out
- These shoes are made for bowling

Cheerleading

- Cheering chicks
- Defying gravity
- Eat, drink, inspire
- Head over heels
- Rah, rah, rah
- Step by step
- Yea, team

Coaching

- A-one coach
- Animal control
- Big plans
- Coaches are goal oriented
- Coaches inspire
- Coaching is an art of the heart
- Inspired by you
- Leading the way
- Listen up
- Little league coach
- Plan B
- Playing by the book
- The master
- Those that love, coach
- Three cheers for coach
- Touching lives
- What a great coach looks like
- When in doubt, inspire
- Words of wisdom
- Work with me
- You're great!
- You're the boss

Diving

Above board
At the water's edge
Defying gravity
Eat, drink, dive
Floating on air
Free falling
Good clean fun
H 2 Ohhhhh
High boy
Hydrotherapy
I came, I saw, I went diving
Jewel of the pool
Man over board
May your board have lots of bounce
Parting the waters
Shockingly refreshing
Sinking to a new level
Slip, slidin' away
Slippery when wet
Soak city
Swimsuit edition
Too cool for the pool
Voyage to the bottom of the pool
Water world
Waterworks
Wet behind the ears
Wicked waters
You rule the pool

Football

Bone crusher
Break pads
Dirt bath
Dirty duds
First down
Football frenzy
Footloose
Friday night lights
Helmet hair/head
It's a kick
Kick off time
Muddy duds
Sunday morning quarterback
Tailgating
The perfect catch

Gymnastics

Air male
Defying gravity
Fly guy
Hang in there
Head over heals
High boy
I can fly
Lord of the rings
Man power
Muscle man
Over the top
Pony boy
Run way
Safety net
Sport's bar
Step by step

Hockey

An interest in ice
Blade runner
Bone crusher
Break pads
Face off
Free checking
Goalies are great
Great save/shot
Helmet hair/head
Hockey heaven
Hockey players are goal oriented
Hockey players are goal setters
Ice king
Net work
Nice shot
On one blade
Open shot
Slap shot
Slip, slidin away
The puck stops here

Soccer

Eat, drink, score
Goalies are great
Great save
Great shot
Net work
Nice shot
Open shot
Soccer players are goal oriented
Soccer players are goal setters

Swimming

At the water's edge
By the big blue water
Different strokes
Eat, drink, wait, swim
Floating fun
Good clean fun
H 2 Ohhhhh
Hydrotherapy
I came, I saw, I went swimming
It's a kick
Jewel of the pool
Parting the waters
Shockingly refreshing
Sinking to a new level
Slippery when wet
Soak city
Son strokes
Stroke smart
Swimming in the fast lane
Swimsuit edition
Too cool for the pool
Water world
Waterworks
Wave runner
Wet behind the ears
Wicked waters
You rule the pool

Tennis

Game point
High ball
Love the game!
May your balls never lose their bounce
Net work
Nice shot/volley
Perfect match
"Racquet"eer

Track and field

Burnin' rubber
Footwork
I came, I saw, I went running
I can fly
Inside track
Leap frog
Marathon man
May your feet fly fast
On the right track

On the run
Quantum leap
Road runner
Run about
Run way
Runners rule
Running wild/with ease
Sports bar

Volleyball

Game point
Gliding light
High ball
Jump/Open shot
Net work

Nice shot/volley
Over the top
Volley girls
What a dig

Weight lifting

Determination
Feel the burn!
Let's see what you can do
Lift master
Man power
Maximum fitness/force
Muscle man

Raise the bar
Sport's bar
The gym is my body shop
The intimidator
Tough man/stuff
World class

Wrestling

Bone crusher
Grudge match
I've been pinned
Man power
Maximum fitness/force

Muscle man
Take down
The intimidator
Wrestling warrior

Wilderness Sports

Appreciates nature
At road's end
Awesome adventure
Back country
Back to nature
Best of the great outdoors
Beyond expectations
Breath of fresh air
Bushwhacking
Communing with nature
Dirt bath/therapy
Dirty duds
Discovering one's self
End of the earth/world
Escape from the ordinary
Escape to _____
Exploring new places
Field and stream
For the love of country
Get out there
God's country
Hidden corners
Hide away
In motion
In search of…..
Into the wild
Land of the lost
Life at it's best
Listening to nature
Magnificent wilderness
Mud therapy
Muddy duds
Nature lover
Off the beaten path
Outer limits
Passport to adventure
Peaceful pastime
Pictures don't lie
Pleasant pursuit
Pure, natural, unspoiled
Rustic retreat
Serenity of the forest
Solitude is sweet
Sounds of silence
Spectacular scenery
Spotting wildlife
Sweet serenity
That's water under the bridge
The _____ wilderness
The good life
The promised land
Uncharted territory
Watching wildlife
Week in the wild
Weekend getaway
What an adventure!
When in doubt, go _____
Wild weekend in the wild
Woodland wonders
Woods and waters

Archery

AA – archer's anonymous
Aim high
All about archery
Archery ace
Arrow dynamics
Arrow head
Bow boy
Bow hunt America
Bow hunter's world
Bulls eye boy
In motion
In search of…..
Lighter than air
May your quiver always be full
Nice shot
Open shot
Quiver king/queen
Sharpshooter
Shootin' time
Stand clear
The master
Tree hunt

Boating

- A day at the lake
- A ship called _____
- All ashore
- Aqua marina
- At the water's edge
- Bay watch
- Blue Lagoon
- Boater's choice/world
- Boating life
- Boats are drift wood
- Bridge over the river_____
- By the big blue water
- Custom machines
- Dockside
- Fantasy island
- Floating fun
- Great lakes, good times
- Land escape
- Lure of the lake
- May your boat always float
- Mysterious island
- Mystic harbor/sea
- On deck
- On still waters
- On the bayou
- On the dock of the bay
- Parting the waters
- Port to port
- Ride like the wind
- River's bend
- River's edge
- Runabout
- Safe harbor
- Sail away
- Sailor boy/girl
- Sailor man/woman
- Sea escape
- Sea quest
- Sitting on the dock of the bay
- That's water under the bridge
- Tranquil harbor
- Wicked\wild waters
- Young riders

Canoeing

- A day at the lake/on the river
- At the water's edge
- Blue lagoon
- Bridge over the river _____
- By the big blue water
- Canoes are drift wood
- Crazy for canoeing
- Dockside
- Eat, drink, float
- Eat, drink, paddle
- Eat, drink, tip over
- Floating fun
- Great lakes, good times
- Land escape
- Lure of the lake
- On still waters
- On the bayou/river
- On the dock of the bay
- On the way to fantasy/ mysterious island
- Paddle power
- Parting the waters
- Ride like the wind
- Riding the rapids
- River's bend/edge
- Safe harbor
- That's water under the bridge
- Tranquil harbor
- We "dugout" the canoe
- Wicked, wild water
- Wild, wet, whitewater
- Young riders

Fishing

A reel nice day at the lake
At the water's edge
Baiting bass/bluegill
Bass master
Big bass
Big reel
Boating life
Boater's choice/world
Boats are drift wood
By the big blue water
Cast away
Cast master
Cast off
Casting for catfish/cod/crappie
Catch all
Catch the moment
Catching catfish/cod/crappie
Custom machines
Dockside
Drag net
Eat, drink, fish, eat
Fish camp
Fish fear me
Fish finder
Fish fun
Fish hunt
Fishing facts
Fishing family/friends
Fishing for flounder
Fishy facts
Fishy family/friends
Fishy tales
Floating fun
Fly-guy
Frying fresh fish
Holy mackerel
Hookin' halibut
Hot line/rod
I came, I saw, I went fishing
I wish I had a fish
King fisher
Line man
Lure of the lake
My rod is my fish stick
Near still waters
Over cast
Pan fish-in'
Parting the waters
Pictures don't lie
Powerful pike
Praying for perch/pike
Reel happiness
Reel pleasures
River's bend
River's edge
Runabout
Safe harbor
Sea hunt
Sea of fishermen
Sea quest
Searching for salmon/sea bass
Snaggin' steelhead/sturgeon
Sneaky snapper
Sun fish-in'
Sword fish-in'
That's water under the bridge
The lure of fishing
The perfect catch
These boots are made for fishin'
Think like a fish
Three little fishies
Thy rod and thy reel, they comfort me
Trophy trout
Trying for tarpon/trout/tuna
Wicked/Wild water

Four Wheeling

Break pads
Breaking away
Burning rubber
Bush whacking
Custom machines
Devil on wheels
Dirt rider
Dirt sports
Easy rider
Fast finish
Faster than a speeding bullet
Faster than the speed of light
Four wheel fanatic
Four wheel fright /fun
Four wheel play/therapy
Freedom in the forest
Got wheels?
Helmet hair
Helmet head
I came, I saw, I went four wheeling
In motion
Inside track
Look at him/her fly
Makin' tracks in the back country
Man and machine
Man over machine
Monster truck
Motor madness/mania
Motor man
Night rider
Noise and toys
Off road adventures
Path finder
Ride like the wind
Rock crawling
Sand trap
Slip, slidin' away
Tearin' up the tread/trail
The drive of your life
Ticket to ride
Trail runner
Trail trek
Young riders
Zoom, zoom, zoom

Hiking

Agony of the feet
Footwork
Freedom of the forest
Happy trails to you
Hiker's haven/heaven
Hiking for good health
Holiday rambler
Not all who wander are lost
Off the beaten path
Packin' light
Pathfinder
Slip, slidin' away
Step by step
These boots are made for hikin'
Trail trek
Uncharted territory

HOT AIR BALLOONS

(FONT: BALLOON XBD BT)

AIR MALE
AIR RIDE
DEFYING GRAVITY
FLIGHT FANATIC
FLIGHT TRAINING
FLOATING ON AIR
FLY GUY
HIGH BOY
I CAME, I SAW, I WENT FLOATING/FLYING

I CAN FLY
INTO THE WILD BLUE YONDER
LIGHTER THAN AIR
LOOK AT ME FLY

RIDE THE WIND
SKY KING
WIND DANCER
WIND SPORT

HUNTING

(FONT: SHOTGUN BT)

AGONY OF THE FEET
BIG GAME BONANZA
BIRD BONANZA
BUCK FEVER
BUCK SHOT
BUCK SKIN
CABIN BOY
CABIN FEVER
COLT 45
BEAR/DEER CROSSING
DECOYING WATERFOWL
DEER SLAYER
DOE SKIN
DUCK TALES
EAT, DRINK, HUNT, EAT
FOOT WORN
FREEDOM OF THE
   FOREST
GUNS AND AMMO
GUN FUN
GUNSLINGER
GUNSMOKE
HAVE GUN WILL TRAVEL
HOPEFUL HUNTER
HUNTER'S PREY
HUNTING BIG GAME
HUNTING FOR _____
HUNTSMAN
I CAME, I SAW, I WENT
   HUNTING
LONE GUNMAN

LONE RANGER
MAGNUM FORCE
MAY YOUR GUN NEVER
   JAM
MIGHTY HUNTER
MONSTER BUCKS
NICE SHOT
OPEN SHOT
PATH FINDER
RABBIT STEW
RIFLE SHOOTER
SHOOTIN' SQUIRREL
SHOOTIN' TIME
STALKING BIG GAME
THE BIG BANG
THE RIFLEMAN
THESE BOOTS ARE MADE
   FOR HUNTIN'
THY GUN AND THY
   BULLETS, THEY
   COMFORT ME
TRAPPER _(NAME)_
TREE HUNT
TURKEYS HUNTING
TURKEYS
VENISON STEW
WATCHING WILDLIFE
WILD GAME DINNER
WOODS AND WATERS
WOODS WALK

Ice Skating

An interest in ice
Baby, it's cold out here
Blade runner
Defying gravity
Dig in
I came, I saw, I went skating
Ice king/queen
On one blade
Peaceful pastime
Slip, slidin' away

Motorcycle/Dirt Bike Riding

Break pads
Breaking away
Burnin' rubber
Call of the open road
Cruisin' in style
Cruisin' on down the road
Custom machines
Defying gravity
Devil on wheels
Dirt bath
Dirt rider
Dirt sports
Dirt therapy
Dirt wheels
Dirty duds
Easy rider
Faster than a speeding bullet
Faster than the speed of light
Full speed ahead
Got wheels?
Helmet hair
Helmet head
High speed
Inside track
Look at him/her fly
Mud therapy
Muddy duds
Night rider
Noise and toys
Off road adventures
Path finder
Pit stop
Race issues
Ride like the wind
Man and machine
Man over machine
Motor fever/mania
Motor madness/mayhem
Motor man
Road and track
Road Racers
Smokin' hot
Speed demon/queen
Tearin' up the tread/trail
The amazing race
The drive of your life
These boots are made for ridin'
Ticket to ride
Trail runner
Victory lane
Young riders
Zoom, zoom, zoom

Rock Climbing

Climb to new heights
Climbers rock
Defying gravity
Dig in
Don't let go!
Hang on!
High boy
Just hangin' out
Path finder
Rock crawling
Rock hound
Slip, slidin' away
Step by step
Sticky fingers
Tent master
Tent time
Uncharted territory
Under the stars

Skydiving

- Air male/ride
- Awesome ride
- Beyond expectations
- Break-neck-n'
- Defying gravity
- Escape from the ordinary
- Fall out
- Floating fun
- Floating on air
- Fly-guy
- Free fallin'
- Get out there
- Hang in there
- Hanging out
- Head over heals
- Helmet hair/head
- High boy/girl/guy
- I came, I saw, I went skydiving
- I can fly
- Into the wild blue yonder
- It's a different world
- Just hangin' out
- Leap of faith
- Look at him/her fly
- Looks like I made it!
- No boundaries
- Outer limits
- Passport to adventure
- Ride the wind
- Sky flying
- Spectacular scenery
- What an adventure
- Wind dance
- Wind sport

Snow skiing

- Baby, it's cold out here
- Dashing through the snow
- Defying gravity
- Dig in
- Floating on air
- Free fallin'
- Frigid air
- Fresh powder
- Full speed ahead
- I can fly
- Lighter than air
- Looks like I made it
- May your skis always be slippery
- Praying for snow
- Sky flying
- Slalom skier
- Slip, slidin' away
- Snow fall
- Snow fever/jump
- Snow goer/seekers
- Snow king/queen
- Snow struck
- These boots are made for skiing
- Uncharted territory
- Wild winter ride

Snowmobiling

- Arctic zone
- Auntie freeze
- Baby, it's cold out here
- Beauty of new fallen snow
- Boots are "snow" shoes
- Cool headed
- Dashing through the snow
- Feeling cold, cold, cold
- Flakes are us
- Freezing family/friends
- Frigid air
- Frosty boy/girl
- Frosty family/friends
- Frozen assets
- Frozen buns/toes
- Frozen family/friends
- Land of the lost
- Praying for snow

Ride like the wind
Slip, slidin' away
Snow blowing
Snow fall
Snow goer/seekers
Snow struck

So little snow
The big chill
Warm up
What's winter without snow?
White wonder
Wild winter ride

Spelunking

Cave color
Cave man/woman
Dig in
Down and dirty
Eat, drink, explore
Hidden treasures
It's a different world
Hangin' in there
Off the beaten path

Pathfinder
Rock crawling
Secret world
Slip, slidin' away
The good earth
The land down under
Uncharted territory
What goes down.....

Surfing

At the water's edge
Beautiful one day, perfect the next
Catch a wave
Free fallin'
Hey dude, where's my board?
Hit the beach/waves
I came, I saw, I went surfing
In the big blue water
Man over board
May your waves all be wicked/wild

Ocean surf
Parting the waters
Ride like the wind
Slip, slidin' away
Surf's up
Surfer dude
The perfect wave
Wave dancer
Wave runner
Wicked/Wild water
Young riders

Water Skiing

At the water's edge
Floating fun
Full speed ahead
Good clean fun
Hit the gas
Hit the lake
Hydrotherapy
In the big blue water
Lure of the lake
Parting the waters

Pure, natural, unspoiled
Shockingly refreshing
Sinking to a new level
Slalom skier
Slip, slidin' away
Slippery when wet
Wave dancer
Wave runner
Wet behind the ears
Wicked/Wild water

Teens

(Font: CAC Futura Casual Bold Italic)

A child no more
Aim high
All grown up
Always be your best
American idol
Anything's possible
Bad boys, bad boys
Bad hair day
Be a leader
Be true to yourself
Beautiful brace face
Believe in the power of your
   dreams
Beyond expectations
Big plans
Bored stiff
Born to be loved
Boy's club
Boy's noise
Brace face
Breath of fresh air
Busy body
Car tunes
Cellular world
Chairman of the bored
Chase your dreams. You may
   catch one!
Child of my heart
Chow down
Chow hound
Claim to fame
Clever girl/guy

Comedy hour
Comic collector's corporate
   office
Comic relief
Complete angels/savages
Computer kid
Conquering the fear of _____
Create tomorrow by what you
   dream today
Curb your enthusiasm
Dangerous age
Dare devil
Dare to be different
Daytime drama
Dear diary
Devil on wheels
Devilishly good looking
Dirt bath
Dirt won't hurt
Dirty duds
Do it best
Do your own thing
Don't knock rock
Dream date
Dude, where's my _____
Dynamic duo
Eat, drink, eat more, drink more
Eight simple rules for raising
   teenagers
Endless energy supply
Every path has a puddle
Exceed your dreams

Fantastic four/five
Feeding frenzy
First born
Food fight
Four teens
Future American idol
Game crazy
Getting together
Giggle fest
Giggling girl
Girl/Guy in the mirror
Girl/Guy next door
Girl/Guy with something extra
Girl's/Guy's club/town
Girls/Guys rock
Girls/Guys on the loose
Girly girls
Give me something good to eat
Going places
Good day sunshine
Good tunes
Got wheels?
Grab life by the tail
Growing pains/up
Growing like a weed
Growth spurt
Guitar man
He's/She's bewitching
He's/She's captivating
He's/She's charming
High maintenance
Hold onto this moment
Hot chicks
Hunk hunter
I look up to you
In search of.....
In style

In your wildest dreams
Inseparable
It's all about you
I've got a secret
I've got nothing to wear
I've got personality
Junior achievement
Just chillin'/hangin' out
Just do it!
Keep him/her safe
Keep learning
Keys to success
Kid rock
King/Queen of cuddle/denial
King/Queen of wishful thinking
Kitchen conversations
Lady's man
Land of the lost
Lead the way
Leave your mark
Less than perfect
Licensed to drive
Life of the party
Like no other
Madhouse
Make a difference
Mall therapy
Mild child
Modern girl
Most wanted
Muddy duds
Music maker/master
My car and my music, they
    comfort me
My car moves me
My cell phone, and my I pod,
    they comfort me

My favorite musician
My turn to drive
My two cent's worth
My world and welcome to it
Never forget your worth
Never give up your dreams
Night owl
No one is better at being yourself than you
No stopping me now
Nobody does it better
Nothing is impossible
Oh, so charming
On the loose
One cannot have too large a party
Our crowd
Party hearty
Party of four/five
Penny for your thoughts
Perfect strangers
Personality portrait
Plan B
Play. It does a body good
Play on
Pure girl/guy
Purely you
Raising dad/mom
Raising the roof
Real teens, real adventures
Realize the power of your dreams
Remarkable you
Road to victory
Rock around the clock
Room for one more
Ruler of the roost
Running wild

Saturday night live
Secret language of teenagers
Secret world of teens
See food, eat it
Set high standards
Shape your future
Shy girl/guy
So many _____, so little time
Some things never change
Sometimes rebellion is a good thing
Sometimes you feel like a nut
Sophistication
Split personality
Stand out in a crowd
Stay off the sidewalk. _____ has his/her driver's license
Stick together
Stomping grounds
Stranger than fiction
Strive for excellence
Sweet stuff
Teen angel
Teen rebel
Teen wisdom
Teenage jungle
That dangerous age
The adventures of _____
The eyes have it
The joker
The joy a teen brings
The lively bunch
The music scene
The next generation
The party's over
Think outside the box
This is me

Thousands of possibilities await you
To tell the truth
Tons of fun
Too much of a good thing
Top dog
Trials and tribulations of teens
Try something new
Tuff stuff
Two/Three girls and a dream
Two/Three girls and a guy
Two/Three guys and a dream
Two/Three guys and a girl
Unique talents
We're outta' here
What a flirt!
What not to wear
What to do with the rest of my life
What's a little dirt?
What's a teenager without a little rebellion?
What's happening?
What's the worst that could happen?
While you were sleeping
Wild cat
Wild weekend
Wired
Yes, Dear
Yes, you can
You and your big ideas
You asked for it
You touch my heart
You want to do what?
You wish
Young Americans
Young ones
Young riders
You-nique
You-niquely you
You're an all star
You're antsy/great
You're worth it!
Youth today
You've got personality
Zonked out

Theater
(Font: Gillies Gothic Ex Bold Shaded LET)

Art from the heart
Can't live without it
Claim to fame
Comic relief
Delightful diversion
Do it best
Do your own thin
Encore, encore
Entertainment tonight
Favorite pastime
For your amusement
For your entertainment
Masterpiece theater

May your passion never wane
New found ability
Passion to perform
Pleasant pursuit
Show of the century
Silver screen dreams
Source of endless pleasure
Stage fright
Theater therapy
True calling
You've got star quality

Travel
(Font: Americana BT)

A wise man travels to discover himself
Admiring the countryside
American express
Another day in paradise
Beyond expectations
Big plans

Break away from the ordinary
Breath of fresh air
Busy bodies
Call of the open road
Can't get enough
Can't live without it

Coast to coast travel
Come away with me
Country travel
Cruisin' in style
Day of departure
Delightful diversion
Do your own thing
Due east/west
Due north/south
Escape from the ordinary
Fantastic journey
Favorite pastime
Follow your heart to the ends of the earth
For the love of country/travel
Foreign travel
From coast to coast
Full speed ahead
Get out there
Globetrotter
Go east/west young man/woman
Go north/south young man/woman
Good eats/times
Green land
Happy trails to you
Hidden corners
Holiday rambler
How far to _____
In motion
In search of...
Incredible views
Journey to _____
Journey to the unknown
Joyful jaunts
Just do it!
Land of the lost
Lead the way
Leaving Las Vegas
Location, location location
Looks like we made it
Miles to go before I sleep
Move forward
New horizons
No boundaries
No one left behind
No stopping me now
North to Alaska
Not all who wander are lost
Not knowing your

destination is half the fun
Off we go
On the loose
Our perfect trip
Outdoor odyssey
Part way to paradise
Passport to adventure
Pit stop
Pleasant pursuit
Ready, set, go!
Roamin' holiday
See the world
Sleeping the miles away
So many destinations, so little time
Spending our children's inheritance
Tales of travel
The incredible journey
The journey is the reward
The quest
Thousands of possibilities await you
Ticket to ride
Touring _____
"Train"ers ride the rails
Travel and leisure
Travel bum
Travel destinations/discoveries
Travel more, work less
Travelers from (hometown)
Travelers from afar
Traveling America
Traveling _____
Traveling the world
Try something new
Uncharted territory
Uneasy rider
We are here
We came from _____
We're getting there
We've come this far
What a beautiful world
What a crazy/wacky world
Where the journey begins/ends
Where to go/stop
Wilderness express
Window to the world
You are here
Young riders
Your ticket to the world
You've come a long way baby

Air travel

A bird's eye view
Air male
Air ride
Air taxi
First class
Flight fanatic
Floating on air
Fly guy

High boy
I can fly
I'll fly away
Into the wild blue yonder
T'was the flight before Christmas
Uncharted territory

Road Trip

A fork in the road
Antiques road show
Are we lost again?
At roads end
Back roads and byways
Bumper to bumper
Car and driver
Country roads
Cruise control
Down the road
Free wheelin'
Got wheels?
Highway to Heaven
Is taking pictures from a moving vehicle, drive by shooting?
Leave the driving to me
Lonesome highways
Motor man

Motoring mishap
My turn to drive
On the road with _____
Passion for the road
Road stories
Road house
Road runner
Roll on
Somewhere down the road
Take the scenic route
The drive of your life
The long road home
The road less traveled
The streets of _____
We've been down this road before
Wheel life
Zoom, zoom, zoom

Vacation

(Font: PosterBodoni BT)

(state) a state of wonder
(your name) in the city
_____ in wonderland
_____ street blues
A new view
A place in the sun
Admiring the countryside
All the comforts of home
Another day in paradise
Assignment _____
At roads end
At the water's edge

Awesome adventures
Back country
Backyard vacation
Bay watch
Beautiful one day, perfect the next
Beyond expectations
Big plans
Blue Hawaii/lagoon
Break away from the ordinary
Breath of fresh air

Bridge over the river _____
By the big blue water
Cabin fever
California dreamin'/dreams
Can't get enough
Can't live without it
City girls/guys
Cityscape
Close to home
Coastal living
Come away with me
Communing with nature
Country cabin
Country destinations
Country discoveries
Country state of mind
Cross roads
Day trippin'
Dazzle your senses
Delightful days/diversion
Discover _____
Discovering one's self
Do something you think you cannot
Do your own thing
Eat, drink, relax
End of the earth/world
Enjoy every moment
Escape from the ordinary
Escape to _____
Experience _____
Exploring new places
Family fun
Family planning
Fantasy island
Far far away
Favorite vacation
Fields forever
For the love of country
Fun while it lasted
Get out there!
Girls on the loose
Girl's/Guy's town
God's country
Good eats
Good morning (state)
Good morning America
Great lakes, good times
Green land
Gullible's travels
Happy days
Have it your way

PU-PON-U MUSTARD MUSEUM

Hidden corners/treasures
Hideaway
Hysterical museum/places
In grand style
In your wildest dreams
Incredible views
Indulge in the things you truly love
Into the wild
It's a different world
It's the pits
Jolly good times
Just hangin' out
Just what the doctor ordered
Land of the lost
Let the games begin
Life at it's best
Lighthouse – a beacon in the night
Little house on the prairie
Living it up at _____
Location, location, location
Log home living
Looks like we made it
Magnificent countryside
Magnificent wilderness
Making the most of now
Mini vacation
Mysterious island
Mystic harbor/sea
Ocean surf
Off the beaten path
Old world charm
On the bayou
On the dock of the bay
On the loose
Opportunity of a lifetime
Outer limits
Path finder
Peaceful pastimes
Picture perfect vacation
Plan B
Play more; work less
Play on
Pleasant pursuit
Pure, natural, unspoiled
Read between the pines
River's bend/edge
Room for one more
Roughin' it easy
Rustic retreat

135

Safe harbor
Seize the day!
Six in the city
Smallville
So many _____, so little time
Somewhere in the night
Source of endless pleasure
Spectacular scenery
Spending our children's inheritance
Spottin' wildlife
Still waters
Tale of two cities
That's water under the bridge
The _____ wilderness
The adventures of _____
The beauty of _____
The great state of _____
The promised land
The sweet life
The vagabonds
They came from _____
Time to move on
Tons of fun
Too much of a good thing
Town and country
Trailer life
Trailer sweet trailer
Try something new
Ultimate adventure/vacation
Uncharted territory
Vacation anticipation
Vacation is the pause that refreshes
Vacation is what you take, when you can no longer take what you've been taking
Vacation romance
Vacation sensations
Vacation vistas
Walking tour
We are here
We came from _____
We say good night to another great vacation
Weekend getaway
Weekend in _____
Weekend in paradise
Weekend warriors
We're outta' here
What an adventure
When in doubt, go on vacation
Wild week/weekend
Wild, wild west
Winter weekend getaway
Woodland wonders
Y'all come back soon
Your ticket to the world

Amusement Parks

Addicted to speed
Chills and thrills
Deadly drop
Face your fears
Family fun
Fast fun
Faster than a speeding bullet
Fly baby, fly
I can fly
I need speed
I walk the line
I'm feelin' wet, wet, wet
In motion
Lights, camera, action
Love those coasters
Midway man/maven/miss/kid
Movers and shakers
On the midway
Park play
Playin' in the park
Ride baby, ride
Ridin' the rides
Roller coaster kid/king/queen
Screaming demons
Showtime
Snack time
Speed is sweet
Speed king/queen/demon
Summer splash

The face of fear
The ice cream was chilling
The wind in your hair
These rides rock

Ticket to ride
Waiting in line
Young riders

At The Beach

(Font: Lambada LET)

A fire in the night
An ocean of sand
At the water's edge
Beach babes/buds
Beach head
Beating the heat
By the big blue water
Coast guard
Coastal living
Cool blue water
Good clean fun
H2Ohhhhh
Hit the beach
Hydrophobia
Hydrotherapy
Just beachin'
Lady in the lake
Near still waters
Ocean surf
Ring of fire
Sand blast
Sand blasters

Sand effects
Sand sculptures
Sand seekers
Sand storm
Sand trap
Sand-emonium
Sea for yourself
Sea you in the summer
Sea you next summer
Seaside
Shell seekers
Soak city
Son and sand
Surfer dude
Surf's up
Swimsuit edition
The big wave
The lure of the lake
The sands of time
The wonder of water
Waterworks
Water world

Camping

(Font: CAC Norm Heavy)

Adopt the pace of nature
Among the trees
Appreciating nature
At road's end
At the river's bend
At the river's/water's edge
Awesome adventure
Back country
Back to nature
Backyard camping
Bear crossing
Beautiful one day, perfect the next
Best of the great outdoors
Beyond expectations
Big plans
Breaking away from the ordinary
Breath of fresh air
Bushwhacking
By the big blue water
Camp more, work less
Camp Run-amok
Camping is a room with a view
Camping life
Can't beat Mother Nature
Can't get enough
Coastal living
Come away with me
Communing with nature
Country life/living
Crazy for camping
Deer crossing
Doing your own thing
Eating out
End of the earth
End of the world
Enjoy the simple things
Escape from the ordinary
Escape to _____
Explore new places
Family fun
Favorite pastime
Finding meaning in the little things
Finding peace within
For the love of country
Gentle country moments
Get out there!
God's country
Going places
Good times
Green land
Have it your way
Hidden corners
Hidden treasures
Hideaway
Holiday rambler
I came, I saw, I went camping
I suffer from OCD – obsessive camping disorder
In search of.....
In the boonies
Indulge in the things you truly love
Into the wild

It's a different world
It's the pits
Just hangin' out
Just what the doctor ordered
Land of the lost
Lead the way
Life at it's best
Listening to nature
Location, location, location
Looks like we made it
Magnificent wilderness
May your bug spray always be handy
Muddy duds
Natural splendors
Nature lover
Nature's beauty
Nature's best
Near still waters
No boundaries
Off the beaten path
Our camper is a mobile home
Our tent is a light house
Our tent is an open house
Our trailer is a road house
Outdoor life
Outer limits
Passport to adventure
Path finder
Peaceful pastimes
Pleasant pursuits
Pure, natural, unspoiled
Read between the pines
Roughin' it easy
Rustic retreat
Serenity of the forest
S'more camping
S'more great moments
So many campgrounds, so little time
Solitude is sweet
Somewhere in the night
Spectacular scenery
Spotting wildlife
Stomping grounds
Sweet serenity
Tent master
Tent time
The __(state)__ wilderness
The great state of _____
The lively bunch
The promised land
The sweet life
The vagabonds
Trail trek
Trailer life
Trailer sweet trailer
Try something new
Tuff stuff
Uncharted territory
Under the trees
Walk among nature
Walk with nature
Watching wildlife
Way out there
We are here
Weekend getaway
Weekend in paradise
Weekend in the wild
Weekend warriors
We're out there
What a beautiful world
What an adventure

What I did on my summer vacation
What's a little dirt?
What's camping without bugs?
What's camping without rain?
When in doubt, go camping
Wild week in the wild
Woodland weekend
Woodland wilderness
Woodland wonders
Woods and waters
Woods walk

Campfires

A fire in the night
All about wood
Burn, baby, burn
Chop sticks
Fire man
Fire woman
I came, I sawed, I warmed up
It's in the pits
Let's marsh-a-mallow
Light my fire
Makin' heat
May your wood always be dry
Plays with matches
Ring of fire
Smokin' hot
Snap, crackle, pop
Some like it hot
Some more s'mores
Something's burning
Somewhere in the night
Tree cutting 101
Tree hunt
Warm up
Wood work

Cruise

(Font: Lasko Even Weight)

A ship called _____
All ashore
Anything's possible
Aqua marina
At the water's edge
Bay watch
Beyond expectations
Big plans
Blue lagoon
Break away from the ordinary
Breath of fresh air
Chase your dreams
Come sail away with me
Crazy for cruising
Cruise America
Cruise control
Dockside

Eat, drink, play
Eat, drink, relax
Eat, drink, shop
Escape from the ordinary
Fantasy island
Favorite vacation
Get out there
Going places
Good eats
Have it your way
I suffer from OCD ~ obsessive cruising disorder
In motion
Indulging in the things you love
It's a different world
Just do it
Land escape
Lead the way
Location, location, location
"Me" time
Move forward
Mysterious island
Mystic harbor/sea
New horizons
North to Alaska
Ocean surf
Never give up your dreams

On the dock of the bay
Parting the waters
Passport to adventure
Port to port
Pursue perfection
Room with a view
Safe harbor
Sailor man
Sea escape
Sea hunt
Sea quest
Seascape
Sitting on the dock of the bay
So many ports of call, so little time
Spending our children's inheritance
Still waters
The lively bunch
Thousands of possibilities await you
Ticket to ride
Tons of fun
Try something new
Young sailors
You're worth it

VOLUNTEERISM

(Font: BankGothic Lt BT)

A lifetime of service
Be a leader
Do more
Get out there
Get things done
Help someone help ones self
Helping others
Leave your mark
Lend a helping hand
Listen to your heart
Make a difference
Make things happen
Nothing is impossible
Shape other's futures
There's a special place in heaven for volunteers
Work together as one

Weather

(Font: Chaucer)

Against the wind
Appreciate Mother Nature
Beautiful one day, perfect the next
Best of the great outdoors
Blue/Dark skies
Breath of fresh air
Climate controlled
Daybreak
Delightful days
Evacuation preparation
Face the wind
Falling water
Feel the rain on your face
Feel the wind in your face
Full moon
Good day, sunshine
Hail of a storm
Harvest moon
Horrible hurricane
How I wish it would rain
Hurricane havoc
Into the wild weather/wind
It's raining, it's pouring
It's the pits
May the weather always be warm
May your days all be sunny
Moonlight madness
Moon shine
Nature's beauty/fury
Northern exposure
Nothing but blue skies
Rainbows apologize for angry skies
Rainbows brighten our world
Red skies at night, sailor's delight
Red skies in the morning, sailors take warning
Safe harbor
Safe haven
Singing in the rain
Still watch
Sun spots
Sunbeams

Terrible tornadoes
Terrible tropical storms
Storm damage
Storm of the century
Storm stories
Storm trackers/watchers
Storm warning
Stormy skies
Summer sun
Sun kissed
Sunset: a great way to end the day
The fury of Mother Nature
The power of Mother Nature
The river's rising
Tornado alley
Under wild skies
Walking in the rain
When it rains, it pours
When the wind blows
Wild weather

Weight

(Font: Futura XBlk BT)

Beauty is in the eye of the beholder
Do your own thing
Don't give up
Don't quit
How's that workin' for ya'?
I did it!
I'm in shape. Round is a shape
I'm not fat, I'm fluffy
I'm not overweight, I'm under tall
Normal is the setting on a dryer
On the loose
One size does not fit all
Pictures don't lie
Sad but true
Self disclosure
Some things never change
Step by step
Take it or leave it
The girl/guy in the mirror
Thin man
This is me
Too much of a good thing
Waist management
"Weight"ing to change
What not to wear
You don't get a body like this by working out
You-nique
You-niquely you

Women

(Font: Cancelleresca Script LET)

A rose between two thorns
A special woman
Bad hair day
Bath and body works
Be confident
Be true to yourself
Beautiful as a rose
Before I was a mom
Believe in magic
Believe in the power
 of your dreams
Bewitching
Beyond expectations
Born to be loved
Breath of fresh air
Busy body
Can't live without them
Captivating
Charming
Chocolatier
Clever girl
Coffee maker
Dear crossing
Do things you think you
 cannot
Dynamic duo
Experience yourself
Fancy/Feminine females
Fantastic four/five
Find peace within
Freaky females
Fun/Funny females
Going places
Good day, sunshine
Gorgeous girls
Have it your way
High hopes
High maintenance
Hunting for a handsome
 hunk
I am woman, hear me
 laugh/cry
I look up to you
In grand style
In search of . . . . .
Indulge in the things you
 truly love

I've got nothing to wear
Inseparable
I've got male
I've got personality
Java time
Kitchen conversations
Life before/after kids
Like no other
Listen to your heart
Love who you are
Love yourself
Lovely legs/lips
Luscious legs/lips
Make yourself heard
Mall therapy
"Me" time
Million dollar woman
Miss/Ms./Mrs. lucky
Modern girl
Most wanted
My beautiful valentine
My sweet valentine
Never forget your worth
Night owl
No one is better at being
   yourself than you
Nothing is impossible
Oh, so charming
One man woman

Party of four/five
Penny for your thoughts
Personality portrait
Pictures don't lie
Play. It does a body good
Purely you
Queen of cuddle
Queen of denial
Queen of good times
Queen of wishful thinking
Realize the power of your
   dreams
Remarkable you
Secret language of women
Self disclosure
Set high standards
Sexiest woman alive
She's the real thing
Smokin' hot!
So many _____,
   so little time
So many kids/men, so little
   aspirin
So much to do, so little energy
Sophistication
Stand out in a crowd
Super girl/human/woman
Sweet thing
That special woman

The beauty of _____
The eyes have it
The girl/woman in the mirror
The girl/woman with
    something extra
The girl/woman who
    changed my life
The lively bunch
This is me
Thy checkbook and thy credit
    card, they comfort me
Tons of fun
Tough stuff
Twilight eyes
Two/Three girls/women
    and a dream
Two/Three girls/women
    and a guy
Unique talents
Va, va, voom

Very much a lady
Wanted: woman
Weary woman
Wicked/Wild woman
What a flirt
What a woman wants
What not to wear
What women like
When you've got it, flaunt it
Wild woman
Wishful/Wistful woman
Woman in training
Woman of the year
Women stick together
Wonderful woman
Yes, you can
You've come a long way baby
You-niquely you
You touch my heart
You're worth it

Woodcutting

(Font: Zurich UblkEx BT)

All about wood
Back to nature
Beaver (name)
Breath of fresh air
Built tuff
Bushwhacking
Busy body
Chain saw champ
Chop sticks
Communing with nature
Determination
Dirty duds
Do it yourself
Forest fighter
Get out there
Grounds work
House warming
Human chainsaw
I came, I sawed, I warmed up
Into the wild
Intriguing trees
King of the forest
Logger head
Makin' heat
Lumber time
Man power
Men in trees
Muddy duds
No stopping it now!
Rustic countryside
Sawing logs
Seek and destroy
Still standing
The intimidator
These boots are made for workin'
Timber craft
Timberrrrr!
Tree cutting 101
Tree hunt
Tuff stuff
Uncharted territory
Walk among nature
What's a little dirt?
Wood work
Woods man
Woods walk

Worship

(Font: BibleScr T)

Acts of faith
Adventures in faith
At home with my faith
Blessed are the believers
Child of God
Christian education
Christian living
Church is God's country
Don't give up on your faith
Faith at work
Faith today
Find peace within
For the love of God
Highway to heaven
Hooked on God
Hope and faith
I love my church
Mass communication
Mass meeting
May your prayers always be answered
Oh come all ye faithful
Our church is prayer conditioned
Prayer circle
Reasons to believe

Safe haven
Soul survivor
The Lord's day
The promised land
True calling

What matters most
When in doubt, pray
Words of faith
Youth worker

Young adults

(Font: Party LET)

Aim high
American idol
Babe magnet
Bad boys, bad boys
Beautiful brace face
Bewitching
Big plans
Born to be loved
Boy toy
Busy body
Captivating
Catchin' some zzz's
Cellular world
Charming
Chick magnet
Chow hound
City girls/guys

Claim to fame
Clever girl/guy
Coffee maker
Comic relief
Cosmo girl
Dangerous age
Dare devil
Daytime drama
Deer crossing
Devil on wheels
Devilishly good looking
Don't knock rock
Dream date
Dude, where's my ___?
Dynamic duo
Endless energy supply
Fastest guitar alive

Feel the beat/heat
Finally legal
Fresh men/women
Future American idol
Game crazy
Getting together
Girls club
Girl's town
Girls/Guys rock
Girly girls
Going places
Good day, sunshine
Good girls/guys
Good tunes
Got wheels?
Guitar man
Hanging out
High maintenance
Honey hunter
Hot blooded
Hot buns
Hot chicks
Hunk hunter
Hunting for a handsome hunk
I look up to you

In grand style
In motion
In search of. . . .
In style
In your wildest dreams
Inseparable
It's all about you
I've got nothing to wear
I've got personality
Java time
Jolly good times
Just chillin'
Keep him/her safe
King/Queen of cuddle/denial
King/Queen of good times
King/Queen of wishful
    thinking
Kitchen conversations
Lady's man
Let the party begin
Letter from home
Life of the party
Like no other
Live out loud
Living single

Looking for love
Love sick
Mad house
Mall therapy
Master of music
Mr./Miss big time
Mr./Miss dreamy/perfect
Mr./Miss lucky
Mod squad
Most wanted
Music makers
My car and my freedom, they comfort me
My car moves me
My favorite musician
My two cents worth
My world and welcome to it
Night owl
No stopping me now
Oh, so charming
On the fast track
On the loose
One cannot have too large a party
Our crowd

Party hearty
Party of four/five
Penny for your thoughts
Personality portrait
Pictures don't lie
Play. It does a body good
Pure girl/guy
Purely you
Remarkable you
Rock around the clock
Rock me baby
Rockin' all night long
Room for one more
Running wild
Saturday night live
Self disclosure
Shy girl/guy
Small town girl/guy
Smokin' hot!
So many girls/guys so little aspirin
So many girls/guys, so little time
Sometimes you feel like a nut
Sophistication

Stud finder
Stud magnet
Stylin'
Super girl/guy
Super hero
Super human
Super man/woman
Sweet stuff
Sweet thing
That dangerous age
The adventures of _____
The eyes have it
The girl/guy in the mirror
The girl/guy with
    something extra
The incredible hunk
The joker
The lively bunch
The music scene
The single life
The wonder of girls/guys
This is me
To tell the truth
Tons of fun
Too much of a good thing

Tuff stuff
Twilight eyes
Two/Three girls/guys and a
    dream
Two/Three girls and a guy
Two/Three guys and a girl
Unique talents
Va, va, voom
We stick together
Weekend warriors
What a flirt!
What not to wear
What to do with the rest of
    my life
What's the worst that
    could happen?
When you're hot, you're hot
When you've got it, flaunt it
Where the wild ones are
Wild cat
Wild life
Wild man/woman
Wild weekend
Wild, wild week
Wired

You and your big ideas
You asked for it
You touch my heart
You want to do what?
You wish!
Young Americans

Young lady/man
You-nique
You-niquely you
Youth today
Zonked out

Zoo

(Font: CAC Moose)

All God's creatures/critters
Amazing animal stories
Amazing animals/alligator/
   aviary
Animal antics/crossing
Animal circus/fair
Anyone want an elephant ear?
Ape antics
Appreciating nature
Aren't I cute?
Awesome alligator/aviary
Baa baa black sheep
Back to nature
Bad boys, bad boys
Beautiful birds
Bear bottom/hug
Big bears
Bird baths
Bless my whiskers
Breath of fresh air?
Bull dozer
Busy bodies
Cagey, aren't you
Cat call/nip/tail
Cat fancier/woman
Catsville

Chickens are "coop"ers
City cats
Cock pit
Comedy hour
Comic relief
Communing with nature
Complete savages
Country cats
Cranky croc
Crazy for cats
Creature comforts/features
Custom home builders
Custom sound
Cute characters/critters
Delightful diversion
Designed by God
Designed by Mother Nature.
   What was she thinking?
Don't feed the animals
Don't touch the animals.
   They may bite
Don't fence me in
Dynamic duo
Eager beavers
Endless energy supply
Escape from the ordinary

152

Everybody's "zoo"in' it
Everything has beauty
Explore your wild side
Family fun
Fancy felines
Fantastic four/five
Father of the pride
Fearfully/Ferociously fun
Feline fever
Flight of the eagle
Flying high
For your amusement/entertainment
Freaky fish
Frighteningly/Frightfully fun
Fun felines
Fun house
Fur face
Good old boys
Grab life by the tail
Growing like a weed
Happy hippos
Have it your way
He got expelled from school. He "cheetah"ed
He got in trouble for "lion"
He got yelled at for "monkey"ing around
Here's the scoop, pick up the poop
High maintenance
Hog haven/heaven
Huge hippos
Hungry, hungry hippo
Hysterical hyenas
I am lion, hear me roar
In motion
In search of.....
Into the wild
It's a different world
It's s"no"w leopard. So, then what is it?

Jungle law
Just hangin' around
Kute kangaroo
Laughable llamas
Lazy lions/lizards
Leader of the pack
Life behind bars
Like no other
Lion's den
Llama mama/papa
Log home living
Lord of the jungle
Mad house
Make yourself heard
Mane event
May your cage always be clean
Miracles from God
Monkey madness
Monkeys are little swingers
Mother Nature's wonders
My world and welcome to it
Nature's beast/best
Newcomer
Night owl
Oh, so charming!
On the loose
On the wild side
Open house
Pack pride
Panda palace
Passport to adventure
Penguin palace/party
Penguins in their tuxes
Planet of the apes
Play boy/girl
Pretty peacocks
Purely you
"Purr"fect pair
"Purr"fectly adorable
Regal eagles
Remarkable reptiles
Remarkable you

Rock crawling/climbing
Room for one more
Running wild
Save the animals
See ya' later, alligator
Silly swimmin' seals
Sleepy sloth
Slithering snakes
Small wonders
Smallville
So many animals, so little time
Source of endless pleasure
Spotting wildlife
Stands out in a crowd
Stomping grounds
Stranger than fiction
Super natural
Tales of the teeth
The eagle has landed
The eyes have it
The incredibles/intimidator
The lively bunch
The real McCoy
The yearling
They came from _____
They came to stay
Tons of fun
Tuff stuff

Two/Three/Four/Five of a kind
Unique talents
Walk among nature
Wary wolves
Watching wildlife
What a pair!
What's a little dirt
What's new for 2009?
When in doubt, go to the zoo
Where the wild things grow
Who's afraid of the big bad wolf
Wild animal babies
Wild cat
Wily coyote
Wired
You ought to be in pictures
"You"nique
"You"niquely you
You're adorable/charming
You're very photogenic
You've got personality
You've got the cutest little _____ face
Zany zebras
Zoo friends/news

Feeding time at the Zoo

All you can eat buffet
Breakfast bar
Chow down/hound
Eating out
Feeding frenzy
Let's eat at the "beast"ro
They're carnivorous

"Let"tuce eat
May your lettuce never wilt
Penguins like the seafood buffet
Salad bar
"See" food buffet
The food is 'ape'tizing

Miscellaneous

(Font: Haettenschweller)

_____ do it better
_____ envy
Blank expressions
Bright idea
Calling all clowns
Can you hear me now?
Delightfully tacky
Do you believe in ghosts?
Everybody's an expert
Food for thought
Get a clue
Give me a break
Good impressions

Lefties do it right
Let it shine
Masquerading as a normal person is exhausting
Out of sight, out of mind
Out of the blue
Passion for purple
Picking up the pieces
Some things never change
There are two sides to every story
Why me?
Will wonders never cease
You asked for it

Descriptive terms

(Font: Times New Roman)

accomplished	angelically	bewitching
active	antsy	big
actively	anxious	bigger
admirable	anxiously	biggest
admirably	appealing	blessed
admiring	appealingly	blessedly
admiringly	appreciative	blooming
adorable	appreciatively	blossoming
adoring	ardent	blushing
adoringly	ardently	blustery
advantageous	arresting	boring
advantageously	artistic	bountiful
adventurous	artistically	bountifully
adventurously	attentive	brainy
affable	attentively	brave
affectionate	authoritative	bravely
affectionately	authoritatively	braver
affluent	available	bravest
afraid	awesome	brawny
ageless	awful	breathing
aggravating	awfully	breathless
aggravatingly	bare	breathlessly
agile	barely	bright
aging	barer	brighter
ailing	barest	brightest
airy	bashful	brightly
alluring	bashfully	brilliant
amateurish	bearable	brilliantly
amateurishly	bearably	brooding
amazing	beautiful	broodingly
amazingly	beautifully	brotherly
amorous	beguiling	bubbly
amorously	believable	busier
ample	believably	busiest
amply	beloved	busily
amusing	benevolent	busy
amusingly	best	buxom
angelic	better	cagey

cagier
cagiest
calm
calmer
calmest
calming
calmly
cantankerous
cantankerously
captivating
carefree
careful
carefully
careless
carelessly
caring
carnivorous
casual
casually
catching
catchy
cautious
cautiously
celebratory
ceremonial
ceremonious
ceremoniously
challenging
changing
charming
charmingly
cheerful
cheerfully
cheerily
cheerless
cheerlessly
cheery
chilling
chillingly
classic
classically
clean
cleaner

cleanest
cleanliest
cleanly
clear
clearer
clearest
clearly
close
closely
closer
closest
cold
colder
coldest
coldly
colorful
colorfully
comfortable
comfortably
comforting
comfortingly
comical
comically
complete
completely
comprehending
comprehensive
confident
confidently
confusing
confusingly
conquering
constructive
constructively
content
contently
controlled
controlling
cool
cooler
coolest
coolly
countrified

courageous
courageously
covert
covertly
cozier
coziest
cozily
cozy
craftier
craftiest
craftily
crafty
crappier
crappiest
crappy
craving
crazier
craziest
crazily
crazy
creative
creatively
creepier
creepiest
creepy
cuddlier
cuddliest
cuddly
cultivated
cultured
curious
curiously
custom
cute
cutely
cuter
cutest
daintier
daintiest
daintily
dainty
dangerous
dangerously

daring	difficultly	early
daringly	dirtier	earnest
darling	dirtiest	earnestly
dashing	dirty	easier
dashingly	disastrous	easiest
dastardly	dumpiest	easily
daunting	disastrously	easy
deafening	discernible	ecstatic
dear	discernibly	ecstatically
dearest	disdainful	edible
dearly	disdainfully	eerie
debonair	diverse	eerily
dedicated	diversely	effervescent
defending	domestic	effervescently
defensive	domestically	efficient
defensively	doting	efficiently
defiant	dotingly	effortless
defiantly	doubtful	effortlessly
definite	doubtfully	elated
definitely	doubtless	elegant
delectable	doubtlessly	elegantly
delectably	drab	elementary
delicious	drabber	elite
deliciously	drabbest	elusive
delightful	drably	elusively
delightfully	dramatic	embarrassing
delirious	dramatically	embarrassingly
deliriously	dreamier	embraceable
depressing	dreamiest	emotional
depressingly	dreamily	emotionally
deserving	dreamy	enabling
desirable	dumb	enamored
desperate	dumber	enchanting
desperately	dumbest	enchantingly
determined	dumbly	encouraging
determinedly	dumpier	encouragingly
developing	dumpy	endearing
devilish	dynamic	endearingly
devilishly	dynamically	endless
devoted	eager	endlessly
different	eagerly	enduring
differently	earlier	energetic
difficult	earliest	energetically

engrossing
enjoyable
enormous
enormously
entertaining
entertainingly
enthusiastic
enthusiastically
erotic
erotically
escaping
eternal
eternally
eventful
eventfully
everlasting
everlastingly
exceeding
exceedingly
excellent
excellently
excitable
exciting
excitingly
exhilarating
expectant
expectantly
expecting
expensive
expensively
experienced
expressive
expressively
extraordinarily
extraordinary
extreme
extremely
fabulous
fabulously
fair
fairer
fairest
fairly

faithful
faithfully
faithless
faithlessly
famous
famously
fanatical
fanatically
fancier
fanciest
fancy
fantastic
fascinating
fascinatingly
fast
faster
fastest
fat
fatherly
fatigued
fatter
fattest
faultless
faultlessly
favorite
fearful
fearfully
fearless
fearlessly
fearsome
fearsomely
feeling
feminine
ferocious
ferociously
fervent
fervently
festive
festively
fierier
fieriest
fiery
filling

final
finicky
first
fit
fitter
fittest
flair
flamboyant
flamboyantly
flavorful
flavorless
flirtatious
flirtatiously
flirty
floundering
flowery
fluent
fluently
fluttering
fond
fonder
fondest
fondly
footloose
forever
forthcoming
fragrant
fragrantly
frantic
frantically
free
freely
fresh
fresher
freshest
freshly
friendlier
friendliest
friendly
frightening
frighteningly
frightful
frightfully

frostier	ghastly	grounding
frostiest	ghostlier	growing
frostily	ghostliest	grueling
frosty	ghostly	gruelingly
fruitful	giddier	grumpier
fruitfully	giddiest	grumpiest
fruitier	giddily	grumpily
fruitiest	giddy	grumpy
fruitless	gigantic	guileless
fruitlessly	gigantically	gullible
fruity	giggling	hairier
frumpier	girly	hairiest
frumpiest	giving	hairy
frumpy	glad	handier
full	gladder	handiest
fuller	gladdest	handily
fullest	gladly	handsome
fully	glorious	handsomely
fun	gloriously	handy
funnier	golden	happening
funniest	good	happier
funny	goodly	happiest
furious	gorgeous	happily
furiously	gorgeously	happy
fussier	grand	harmonious
fussiest	grander	harmoniously
fussily	grandest	haughtily
fussy	grandly	haughty
futuristic	grateful	healthful
gallant	gratefully	healthier
gallantly	great	healthiest
generous	greater	healthily
generously	greatest	healthy
genius	greatly	heartfelt
gentle	gregarious	heartier
gentlemanly	gregariously	heartiest
gentler	grieving	heartily
gentlest	griping	heartless
gently	groovier	heartlessly
genuine	grooviest	hearty
genuinely	groovy	heavenly
ghastlier	groping	helpful
ghastliest	grounded	helpfully

heroic
heroically
hidden
high
higher
highest
highly
hilarious
hilariously
hip
hipper
hippest
historical
historically
homelier
homeliest
homely
homemade
honorable
honorably
hopeful
hopefully
hopeless
hopelessly
horrible
horribly
horrific
horrifically
hostile
hot
hotly
hotter
hottest
huge
hugely
huggable
humorous
hungrier
hungriest
hungrily
hungry
hurried
hurriedly

hurtful
hurtfully
hysterical
hysterically
humorous
humorously
idealistic
idealistically
identical
identically
ill
illuminating
illuminatingly
illustrious
illustriously
imaginative
imaginatively
impossible
impossibly
impressionable
improving
incredible
incredibly
incredulous
incredulously
indulgent
indulgently
industrial
infatuating
innocent
innocently
innovative
inseparable
inseparably
insightful
inspirational
inspiring
intelligent
intelligently
intense
intensely
interesting
interestingly

intriguing
iridescent
irregular
irregularly
irritable
irritably
irritating
irritatingly
isolated
jauntier
jauntiest
jauntily
jaunty
jazzy
jealous
jealously
jointly
joking
jokingly
jollier
jolliest
jolly
joyful
joyfully
joyless
joylessly
joyous
joyously
jubilant
jubilantly
justifiable
justifiably
kind
kinder
kindest
kindly
kissable
knowledgeable
lankier
lankiest
lanky
large
largely

larger	louder	mean
largest	loudest	meaningful
lasting	loudly	meaningfully
lastingly	lovable	meaningless
latest	lovably	meaninglessly
laughable	lovelier	meanly
laughably	loveliest	melancholy
lavish	lovely	melodious
lavishly	loving	melodiously
lazier	lovingly	memorable
laziest	loyal	memorably
lazily	loyally	merely
lazy	luckier	merrier
lean	luckiest	merriest
leaner	luckily	merrily
leanest	lucky	merry
least	lucrative	messier
leery	lurid	messiest
leisurely	luscious	messily
level	lusciously	messy
light	lustful	mild
lighter	lustfully	milder
lightest	luxurious	mildest
lightly	luxuriously	mildly
limited	mad	mindful
limitless	maddening	mindfully
listless	maddeningly	mini
listlessly	madder	minutely
little	maddest	miraculous
littler	madly	miraculously
littlest	magical	mischievous
loftier	magically	mischievously
loftiest	magnificent	modern
loftily	magnificently	moodily
lofty	malleable	moody
long	manageable	mortal
longer	manly	mortally
longest	marvelous	motherly
loose	marvelously	mountainous
loosely	massive	mournful
looser	massively	mournfully
loosest	masterful	mousy
loud	masterfully	moving

movingly	observantly	personable
muddier	obsessive	pitiful
muddiest	obsessively	pitifully
muddy	odorous	plausible
muscular	ogling	plausibly
muscularly	old	playful
mushy	older	playfully
naive	oldest	pleasant
naively	open	pleasantly
natural	openly	pleasing
naturally	opportunistic	pleasingly
naughtily	opportunistically	pleasurable
naughty	optimistic	plump
neat	optimistically	plumper
neater	opulent	plumpest
neatest	opulently	pointless
neatly	ordinarily	pointlessly
neighborly	ordinary	poor
new	ornerier	poorer
newer	orneriest	poorest
newest	ornery	poorly
newly	outgoing	portlier
nice	overbearing	portliest
nicely	overt	portly
nicer	overtly	possibly
nicest	overzealous	potent
nimble	painful	potently
noisier	painfully	powerful
noisiest	passionate	powerfully
noisily	passionately	powerless
noisy	peaceful	powerlessly
notable	peacefully	prayerful
notably	perennial	prayerfully
notorious	perennially	precious
notoriously	perfect	preciously
nurturing	perfectly	pretentious
oblivious	perkier	pretentiously
obliviously	perkiest	prettier
obnoxious	perky	prettiest
obnoxiously	permanent	prettily
obscure	permanently	pretty
obscurely	persistent	priceless
observant	persistently	privileged

professional	ravenously	romantic
professionally	ravishing	romantically
promising	ravishingly	rough
proper	readily	rougher
properly	ready	roughest
prosperous	real	roughly
prosperously	really	rowdier
proud	rechargeable	rowdiest
prouder	recognizable	rowdily
proudest	regal	rowdy
proudly	regally	rude
pure	regional	rudely
purely	regionally	ruder
purer	relaxed	rudest
purest	relentless	rushed
quaint	relentlessly	rustic
quaintly	relevant	sad
queenly	relevantly	sadder
queer	religious	saddest
queerer	religiously	sadly
queerest	remarkable	safe
queerly	remarkably	safely
querulous	reminiscent	safer
querulously	resourceful	safest
quick	resourcefully	saintlier
quicker	restful	saintly
quickest	restfully	sappier
quickly	restless	sappiest
quiet	restlessly	sappy
quieter	reverent	sassier
quietest	reverently	sassiest
quietly	revolutionary	sassy
quirkier	rich	satiny
quirkiest	richer	satisfied
quirky	richest	satisfying
radical	richly	satisfyingly
radically	righteous	saucier
rambling	righteously	sauciest
rapt	rigorous	saucily
raptly	rigorously	saucy
rapturous	riskier	savage
rapturously	riskiest	savagely
ravenous	risky	savory

savvier	shiniest	smooth
savviest	shiny	smoothly
savvy	sick	snide
scandalous	sicker	snidely
scandalously	sickest	soapier
scarier	sickly	soapiest
scariest	silky	soapy
scarily	sillier	soaring
scary	silliest	social
scenic	silly	socially
scenically	simple	soothing
scrappier	simpler	soothingly
scrappiest	simplest	sophisticated
scrappy	simply	soulful
scratchy	sincere	soulfully
scrumptious	sincerely	sound
scrumptiously	sinful	soundly
seasoned	sinfully	sparkling
secretive	sisterly	sparkly
secretively	skillful	special
seductive	skillfully	spectacular
seductively	skinnier	spectacularly
sensational	skinniest	spicy
sensationally	skinny	spirited
sensitive	sleepier	spiteful
sensitively	sleepiest	spitefully
sensual	sleepily	spookier
sensually	sleepy	spookiest
sensuous	slight	spooky
sensuously	slighter	squeezable
sentimental	slightest	stealthy
sentimentally	slightly	steely
serene	slim	sterile
serenely	slimmer	stickier
serious	slimmest	stickiest
seriously	slippery	sticky
sexier	small	still
sexiest	smaller	stillest
sexy	smallest	stirring
shapelier	smart	stirringly
shapeliest	smarter	stormy
shapely	smartest	strange
shinier	smartly	strangely

stranger	tamest	tinier
strangest	tantalizing	tiniest
stressed	tantalizingly	tiny
strictly	tasteful	tired
striking	tastefully	tiredly
strikingly	tastier	tolerant
striving	tastiest	tolerantly
strong	tasteless	touchable
stronger	tasty	touchier
strongest	taut	touchiest
strongly	tauter	touchy
struggling	tautest	tough
stupid	tautly	tougher
stupidly	tearful	toughest
successful	tearfully	trainable
successfully	tempting	trained
suffering	temptingly	treasured
super	tender	tremendous
superb	tenderly	tremendously
superbly	terrible	trite
superficial	terribly	true
superficially	terrific	truer
superfluous	terrifically	truest
superlative	testier	truly
supple	testiest	trusted
suppler	testily	trusting
supplest	testy	trustworthy
surprised	thinking	twinkling
surprising	thirstily	twisted
surprisingly	thirsty	unbelievable
surviving	thoughtful	unbelievably
sustainable	thoughtfully	uncomfortable
sweet	thoughtless	uncomfortably
sweeter	thoughtlessly	unconditional
sweetest	thrilled	unconditionally
sweetly	thrilling	understanding
sympathetic	thrillingly	understandingly
sympathetically	thunderous	unique
tactful	thunderously	uniquely
tactfully	timeless	uplifting
talented	timelessly	upsetting
tame	timid	urban
tamer	timidly	urgent

urgently
vain
vainly
valiant
valiantly
valuable
vast
vastly
velvety
vicarious
vicariously
victorious
victoriously
vivacious
vivaciously
voracious
voraciously
wanting
warily
warm
warmer
warmest
warmly
wary
watchful
watchfully

wearier
weariest
wearily
weary
well
wet
wetly
wetter
wettest
whimsical
whimsically
wholesome
wholesomely
wild
wilder
wildest
wildly
winning
winningly
wired
wise wisely
wiser
wisest
wishful
wishfully
wistful

wistfully
womanly
wonderful
wonderfully
wondrous
wondrously
worrisome
worthwhile
worthy
wretched
wretchedly
yielding
young
younger
youngest
youthful
youthfully
zanier
zaniest
zany
zealous
zealously
zestful
zestfully
zippy

YOUR FAVORITE TITLES

PAGE IDEAS

Made in the USA
Lexington, KY
14 March 2012